NO MEMORIAL

NO MEMORIAL

*The Story of a Triumph of Courage
over Misfortune and Mind over Body*

ANTHONY BABINGTON

LEO COOPER

First published 1954 by William Heinemann Ltd

Re-published by Leo Cooper Ltd 1988

Leo Cooper is an independent imprint of
the Heinemann Group of Publishers
10 Upper Grosvenor Street, London W1X 9AP

LONDON   MELBOURNE   AUCKLAND

ISBN 0-85052-074-6

Printed and bound in Great Britain by
Biddles Ltd, Guildford and King's Lynn

Dedicated to
The war–disabled of all nations
and to
All those who have helped them

PUBLISHERS' NOTE

THIS book tells the story of one man's struggle to overcome the effects of extremely serious head wounds, sustained when serving with the Army in Holland, and of his fight to retake his place in ordinary life.

It therefore seems appropriate to say a few words about the development of neurosurgery both before and after the outbreak of the Second World War. In the first place it should be borne in mind that in the First War the mortality rate from penetrating head wounds was 90 per cent. Few surgeons had any knowledge of the treatment of such wounds and the casualties were, in the main, looked after by general surgeons with no specialized skills. In the Second World War the statistics were reversed and 90 per cent of the patients who reached neurosurgical units survived. Clearly great progress had been made in the intervening years, and for this much of the credit is due to one man—Hugh, later Sir Hugh, Cairns.

In 1916 Dr Harvey Cushing, the great American pioneer of neurosurgery, had brought over a small unit to France, dedicated to the treatment of head wounds. Cairns, as a young surgeon, spent a year in Boston with Cushing after the war, an experience which determined him to specialize in neurosurgery. In the mid-1930s Lord Nuffield had decided that the introduction of clinical professorships at the Radcliffe Infirmary, in close association with the University of Oxford, was necessary to improve the standard of local medical care and in 1937 Cairns was appointed to the new Chair of Surgery, at the same time acting as Consultant Neurosurgeon to the Army. In 1939, when it became plain that another war was inevitable, the War Office took over St Hugh's College, Oxford, near the Radcliffe, as a Military Hospital for Head Injuries. Between

vii

1940 and 1945 in this hospital of 300 beds some 13,000 patients from the Army, the RAF, the Royal Navy and the Allied Forces were treated for spinal as well as head injuries. Here also was provided an excellent training ground for neurologists, neurosurgeons, nurses and orderlies, who served in every theatre of war and saved countless lives.

In all campaigns it became clear that effective segregation of head cases depended to a very great extent on air evacuation. Sooner or later in all major theatres of war, 90 per cent of patients with head wounds were in the hands of experts, fully equipped neurosurgeons, at distances varying from 10 to 1,000 miles from the front, in time to have their wounds completely closed after excision and cleaning; the majority were operated on within forty-eight hours of injury. In over 90 per cent of those who survived the initial brain damage, wounds healed by first intention. Brain fungus became a rare event and the death rate from infection in penetrating brain wounds was reduced to 5 per cent, or less. In non-penetrating wounds the death rate was under 1 per cent, and when there were no neurological signs the patients returned to duty often without leaving the Army area.

St Hugh's and the Radcliffe, however, remained the focal point on which neurologists and neurosurgeons from all over the world converged to learn and to discuss the best forms of treatment and rehabilitation, and it was to St Hugh's that Anthony Babington came in October, 1944. He had sustained a severe penetrating wound, involving the left hemisphere of the brain, mainly in the left temporal region. After a brilliant operation by Colonel Cecil Calvert, his wound healed without complication. However, the right side of his body was paralysed and he was mute. It is worth noting that at the time there were no trained speech therapists and Sir Hugh Cairns had to rely upon "amateurs", though they were, in fact, highly successful. Violet Brooks, who taught the author to speak again, had been a singing teacher before the war. After some weeks he was able to produce a few sounds, and his right leg improved rapidly with physiotherapy. On the other hand the function in his right arm and hand remained severely impaired. Gradually, with intensive speech therapy, he was able to relearn words like a child. Three and a half years' later he was able to pass his bar final examinations and, happily, retained the urge to do his best in life. Frequently penetrating wounds of this type destroyed the patients' "drive" and they gave up the struggle to return to a normal life.

Although Babington was right-handed and therefore the speech function was in the left hemisphere of his brain, speech therapy enabled him to learn to speak with the right hemisphere. It is known that in about 10 per cent of patients speech is bilaterally represented sufficiently for this "miracle" to occur. A surgeon who saw the nature of his wound at the time has said that there was no way that speech could have been relearned with the left temporal lobe. Fortunately, his intellect and personality were unblemished, and epilepsy, which affects 40 per cent of patients with penetrating wounds, did not supervene.

However, as the reader will learn, the road to recovery was long and painful and all the medical skill in the world could not have succeeded had not Tony Babington been brave enough, or lucky enough, to hang on to that indomitable will to overcome his handicaps which is reflected in every page of his book.

AUTHOR'S NOTE

WHEN I was writing *No Memorial* almost thirty-five years ago I was endeavouring to describe, while my recollections were still vivid and clear, my initial experiences after being severely wounded in the head during the autumn of 1944. I had always hoped that my account would be published anonymously; that is why I concealed the identities of all the people in the story. If I had foreseen that the book was destined to appear under my name I have no doubt that I would have been reluctant to reveal my thoughts and my feelings in the way I have done.

On re-reading these pages, after so many years, it was natural that I should have wanted to make changes—perhaps an opinion or comment expressed which I had later regretted; perhaps an omission which I now wish to rectify; perhaps a passage which could have been better expressed. However, Leo Cooper, my publisher, and I both agree that any editing at this stage might impair the frankness and the spontaneity of what I had written in the first place, and that, therefore, the original text should remain unaltered in this edition.

There is one error which I would like to correct. On page 145 I refer to the Queen (now Queen Elizabeth the Queen Mother) dining in the Middle Temple as a "guest". She was then, and still is, a most loved and revered Bencher of the Inn and was, of course, attending the dinner in that capacity.

Anthony Babington
Chilham
Kent

"There be of them, that have left a name behind them,
That their praises might be reported.
And some there be, which have no memorial;
Who are perished, as though they had never been born."
(Ecclesiasticus. Chapter 44)

PROLOGUE

VICTOR had always loved to wander through fields of ripening corn. He told me once that they were so clean and virile they filled his soul with poetry.

"Sometimes," he said, "when I have stood and stared at a cornfield for a long time I imagine I am looking at a silent army of pensive crusaders. And then the light changes suddenly and I am only aware of the beautiful freshness of untarnished youth."

Perhaps what he was really seeing was a reflection of his own magnificence, for Victor possessed more of the elements of perfection than anyone I had ever met. He was young, handsome, strong, intelligent and charming. He had known early in his life what it was to have the whole world at his feet. At school and at the university every door had opened to his touch. After the war it would be the same, we thought. Nothing could stem his triumphal progress.

But those of us who were closest to Victor knew that he had one grave weakness. His mind was perpetually obsessed with a single fear—the dread of growing old.

He used to say, "There is nothing fine about old age and senility. There is a right time to die—Shelley realised that —in a moment of ecstasy and without pain. It comes when you have climbed to the summit of the mountain, but before you have commenced to descend."

I was with him throughout his active service and I often thought his philosophy was the cause of his intrepid courage. Again and again he emerged unscathed from the fiercest engagements and his valour was rewarded with decorations and promotions.

Then he developed a new horror.

"I often have a nightmare," he once told me. "And in it

I am walking down the road with an artificial leg or with a sleeve of my jacket hanging empty at my side." He shuddered. "Please God, it will never happen like that. It wouldn't be worth going on living; I think I would put an end to myself."

His worries were unnecessary. The sniper's bullet was sure, swift, and merciful.

They called me to the place as soon as they could get hold of me. Victor was lying at the side of one of those sunken cart-tracks which wind like knotted veins throughout the Bocage country in Normandy. He who had been so radiant in all the vitality of life was now frigid and barren in the emptiness of death. All around stretched out the close-sown acres of golden corn which he had once loved.

We buried him a short while after I had arrived. At first I was appalled by the awful tragedy that his manifold gifts were to be so wantonly scattered forever in some remote corner of an alien battlefield. Later, however, I realised that this was the death he had ardently desired, and it had come some time before he had been compelled to start on the long, slow descent on the far side of the mountain.

Now he would be remembered in all the glory and the faultlessness of his young life. A star which had hung a second or two in dazzling brilliance before vanishing for all eternity into the immeasurable vaults of the heavens.

And the world remained with us who were left.

CHAPTER I

SUDDENLY there was a shell overhead louder than the rest; a mad, tempestuous, frenzied searing of the air; an agonised screeching inevitability. A fragment of a second, with realisation coming too late for action. And then a fearful, crushing nothingness.

I opened my eyes and tried to reorientate my swimming senses. There was a loud buzzing in my head. I fought hard to come to, but I was wedged in the first fleeting, transitory state of returning consciousness.

Even then, I was able to marshal my thoughts. A shell had exploded near me, I thought. I had been stunned by the blast. I had been accidentally knocked out several times before on various playing fields so I should have been treading familiar paths. This, however, was different. I ought to be returning quickly, as a lantern-slide finding focus, instead of which I was floating above my body with no connecting links of control or feeling.

Footsteps running and Sergeant-Major Nicholls bending over me looking anxious and worried:

"Are you all right, sir?"

And then quickly turning his head and shouting over his shoulder:

"Stretcher-bearers! Quickly! Stretcher-bearers!"

I wanted to tell him I was unhurt, only stunned. That I must rest for ten minutes and I would be fully recovered. I found I had no idea how to talk. I made a supreme effort to re-enter my body, but I continued to float aimlessly above it, as listless and uncontrollable as a small boat drifting idly on its moorings.

Nicholls took off his greatcoat and put it over me. More footsteps. A stretcher thrown on the ground. Men kneeling beside me trying to prop me up. Doing some-

1

thing to my head. Then silence and an intense loneliness.

The idea, deliberately pushed into the back of my mind, broke loose from the shadows and stood before me, gaunt and frightening. I tried to fight it back unsuccessfully; it was terrifying in its size and clarity, and saying to me: "Something is wrong, very wrong. You have never encountered anything like this before. You are not merely stunned; it is a lot worse."

I had heard of men being knocked unconscious by blast; being badly hurt; even dying. It seemed hard to have to fight these fears alone with nobody to confide in or talk to. I seemed to have been abandoned and the early dawn was breaking over the sodden Dutch countryside. I felt like a sick dog must feel when it is shut up alone in the kitchen.

Once someone came and tried to make me drink a mug of tea, but I could not co-operate and it slopped from my lips on to my neck.

I began to pray; a simple, repeated prayer that, whatever was wrong with me, I would get better. I wanted even a vague feeling of normality to free me from this uncomfortable plane of existence on which I had landed. It occurred to me that I was dead and my soul was lingering by my body before it started on its journey. I rejected that theory quickly. I was not dead, but probably I was dying, and at that moment death appeared to me as a final snuffing out of life and light and passing into a dark, timeless vacuum.

At last there were people all round me. Orders, movement, instructions.

They put me on to a stretcher and lifted it up. Then the uneven pulling, jolting as they walked.

I knew I was holding on to life by a single thread; that if I closed my eyes and relaxed it would be the finish. I must hold on and fight even though I dearly longed to enter the door which opened so invitingly before me; everything I desired was there; peace, quiet, coolness and oblivion. But once having entered there would be no return.

They transferred me to a stretcher slung across the hood

2

supports on a jeep. Corporal Huggins, the N.C.O. in charge of the company stretcher-bearers, balanced himself standing beside me. He tucked a blanket round me and from time to time murmured words of reassurance.

I could hear Sergeant-Major Nicholls' voice, still arranging, still ordering. I wanted to say good-bye to him, as he was one of the finest men I had ever met. I knew it was useless. I realised I had already severed contact with everything we had experienced and shared together. The jeep drove away without his coming near me again.

By now it was becoming quite light. Shells were landing in the fields on either side of the road. A few German Spandau machine-guns were firing tracer into our positions, hysterical, jabbering, stammering, and dotted lines of coloured bullets flew over us.

"It's all right, sir. They're firing high. We'll be all right." Huggins kept up his friendly monologue.

The Regimental Aid Post was in a barn about a mile behind our front line. I was carried in and laid on a wooden trestle table. Soon the Medical Officer and a couple of orderlies were bending over me, examining my head. They appeared to be doing something and they spoke to each other in undertones while they worked.

Now and then I picked up what they were saying:

Someone spoke of something 'oozing'.

And then the doctor:

"I'm afraid I can't do much for him. Is the road clear, Sergeant?"

The sergeant leaned over me.

"Can he hear?"

"No," said the doctor, "he's clean out."

"The road is passable, but it's under very heavy fire. Are you going to send him back?"

"Why not? He's still alive."

"There's only one ambulance left."

"I'll have to risk it. We must give him a chance even if it's a very slender one."

3

"That will leave us with not a single ambulance. He doesn't look as though he'd ever make it."

The doctor's voice receding in the distance:

"He's still living. We must give him a chance."

Again they left me to my desperate solitude. I was feeling worse. Not pain, because I was beyond pain. Not ill, for that is too definite and definable a sensation. Discomfort would be a gross under-description; this was a hundred times worse than the greatest discomfort I had ever suffered. And all the time that feeling that my strength was ebbing away. But I knew that I must hold on; like a half-drowned man clutching a piece of floating débris without any finger-holds. I wondered if it was worth while continuing to fight; whether death would be the inevitable outcome; whether I, like a cornered animal, was resisting instinctively in the last blind, unreasoning frenzy when everything is cleared from its mind except a primitive, lunatic desire of self-preservation.

So I continued to pray endlessly that I might become well again.

They came in with a stretcher and carried me outside. Everything tilted, then creaks and groans, and I was inside the ambulance. The door slammed, the engine revved; we started forward joltingly along the rough road.

I could not hold on any longer; I struggled and then gave up. The white roof of the ambulance became streaky; a distant sound welled up inside me. And then a black silence.

I came to several times. I was always lying alone and always we were crawling along, bumping, jerking, braking and re-starting. I could hear other vehicles passing and, occasionally, hoarse shouts.

My mind was working things out logically and sensibly all the time, but my brain seemed to have a separate existence from my body, which was not really mine any more.

'They are leaving me alone,' I thought, 'because they can

4

do nothing for me. For the present I am the only one who can save myself by deliberately staying alive. Later, if I can fulfil my part, others will take over from me and I will be able to relax.'

Once when I became conscious the situation was different. My stretcher was on a concrete floor in a long, narrow room; other men on stretchers were lined up on either side so close that we were almost touching one another. An officer with R.A.M.C. flashes was working along the line taking notes. When he came to me he examined a label tied to my tunic. He straightened up and shouted some orders which I did not understand. Presently more people appeared and I was carried out.

It was clear daylight by now and the sun was shining brightly. I noticed how quiet the atmosphere was and judged that we must be a good distance behind the line.

An ambulance was waiting outside. The ritual was repeated; orders, grunts and rattling. The door banged and we started on our way once more.

I have no idea how long I spent travelling in ambulances. I noticed during my periods of consciousness that I was becoming progressively worse. It was not that my faculties were becoming in any way clouded; indeed my perception remained clear and my reason comparatively lucid. It was just as though my connection with my physical person was becoming increasingly remote; as if I was passing through the phase between daylight and darkness, when the ebbing afterglow obstinately persists in holding at bay an utter blackness. As I swayed between being and not-being I felt that my moments of consciousness were becoming shorter and less frequent.

I was hazily aware of the passing of time, although the inside of the ambulance was blacked out and the dim light embedded in the ceiling always appeared to shine with the same feebleness.

And still the journey continued until waking and sleeping became jumbled and confused into one endless night-

5

mare. Whenever I speculate now on what horrors hell might contain to torment a captive soul my mind invariably recalls that timeless ambulance journey, imprisoned and in solitary confinement.

I have a dim recollection of finding myself on a trolley being wheeled along a corridor, khaki figures walking on either side, and a nurse in clean, fresh uniform looking down on me. I think I must have given some sign of recognition, because she smiled and put her hand on my forehead.

"You're in hospital in Brussels," she said. "We're going to make you better."

She was the first person who had troubled to speak to me, it seemed, since soon after it had all begun, and I felt very grateful. The supreme loneliness of semi-consciousness is almost inconceivable if you have never experienced it. Such loneliness, I think, as must be felt by a spirit returning invisibly to once-familiar places and passing unnoticed amongst once-loving friends.

They took me into a very small room containing one bed. There they undressed me, but it was as though they were undressing another person. Everybody left the room except the nurse; she continued to do things and then drew the curtains together.

Standing at the foot of my bed she regarded me intently and said:

"I wonder if you can understand what's happening? If you can hear me," she spoke slowly and deliberately, "relax and don't worry. You are going to sleep now."

I am not sure whether or not she gave me an injection before she left the room.

It was pitch dark and very quiet. I wondered if they had brought me there to die.

Either I fell asleep or else I slipped into the shadowed recesses of unconsciousness, for the next thing I knew was the door opening noisily. The light was switched on and the nurse walked in, followed by a crowd of orderlies.

She came up to me again and said:

"You are being flown back to England. You will recover there."

As they were lifting me on to a trolley I passed out.

When I opened my eyes I was once more alone in the back of an ambulance. On the whole I felt slightly better; as though something had given me additional strength, although my mind was still working without any connection to my body.

They were going to fly me home, I thought; that meant there was definite hope. Someone had told me once that they were flying all the very badly wounded straight back to England and that a number died on the plane, but the remainder, having surviving the journey, usually recovered. At last I saw a time-limit to my struggle. I was suddenly convinced that if I was able to hang on until the plane landed in England I might then relax because the danger would be over.

The sound of the wheels altered as though we were leaving a rough gravel path and travelling over a field—to judge from the jolts, an uneven one. Was this the airfield?

There followed a tedious period, crawling, shunting, and reversing, accompanied all the while by hoarse, meaningless shouts.

Eventually the bolts were drawn back and the doors thrown open in a burst of daylight. As they lifted out my stretcher I became aware of a plane close at hand; I did not see it exactly, as my eyes were staring up at the clouded sky, but I sensed the dark object towards which I was being carried.

All of a sudden the sky was blotted out by a roof. A female voice with an American accent was giving instructions. The roof was drawing closer and I closed my eyes. Then all movement ceased.

I opened my eyes again and took in where I was. The plane had a gangway running up the centre; on either side was a double row of bunks, one above the other. I was in

7

a top bunk on the right-hand side. A pretty, dark girl in American service dress was beside me; as she stood in the gangway I was level with her head and shoulders.

She spoke in a soft, musical voice:

"Are you comfortable now?"

I wanted to tell her that I was all right, but I had no idea how to speak.

She looked puzzled.

"You want something, I know you want something. Can't you tell me what it is?"

She paused watching my face searchingly.

Someone in a bunk opposite called out. She brightened.

"Of course, that's it. You want a cigarette. How stupid of me not to have guessed."

She put a cigarette into her mouth and lit it. Then she stuck it between my lips. I could not feel anything, and in any case I did not want to smoke. She grabbed the cigarette as it fell on to my chest. Then she stayed for a few minutes, her large, kind eyes close above mine.

"I want to help you, Officer," she said, "but you won't speak and tell me what it is you want. I must leave you now as I've got other things to do, but I'll be spending a lot of time with you on the trip, so don't worry about it."

She went away and I saw the man in the top bunk across the way. He was a stocky, bull-necked fellow and he was sitting up looking thoroughly pleased with himself. He kept up a constant stream of conversation in a humorous Cockney accent. Every now and again I could hear a roar of laughter at one of his sallies, but I did not catch what he was saying.

'I must hold on during the journey,' I was thinking; and then a prayer. 'Please God, lend me strength to hold on.'

Suddenly I felt my bunk heaving and tilting beneath me as though some Hercules had grabbed up the end and was shaking it in a spasm of vicious fury.

It was a few moments before I realised that we had started. I realised too how great a trial was in store for me

8

as my discomfort was greatly increased by the pitching and jolting.

The American nurse came up:

"Don't worry. You'll get used to the motion of the plane presently. Every minute's taking you nearer home."

I wanted her to stay beside me talking, as it made things easier.

Her face became dimmed and blurred. I heard her saying: "Steady, old chap! Steady!" She seemed to be a long way away. Then she was no more.

During that air trip I was out most of the time. There were, however, innumerable occasions when I regained consciousness for fleeting moments, but even at such times I never became completely aware of my surroundings. Invariably the American was there speaking soft, comforting words which were unintelligible; sometimes I saw her face mistily as through a veil.

Only once did I recover at all fully. I found myself trying to lean over the side of the bunk; then I was sick. Immediately the Cockney shouted for help and the nurse ran up. As she was pushing me back gently, I was surprised to see that my pillow was soaked in blood. As usual she stayed by my side for a bit.

There was something cold, uncomfortable, and stiff along my right side. I puzzled over it for a while before it dawned on me that it was my right arm, frigid, impersonal, and paralysed. I took in the fact without alarm or surprise and drifted off into the haze of oblivion.

The next thing I knew was that all motion had ceased. My stretcher was lying on the floor of the gangway and all the bunks, as far as I could see, were empty. The American nurse was kneeling beside me tucking a blanket round my neck.

"Well, you're in England now. You'll soon be safe and sound in bed in hospital. I reckon it's time to say good-bye."

She sat back on her heels.

9

"I hope you'll be all right. You look a good sort. I like you."

She put a cool hand on my cheek and left it there.

Next I was in bed in a room which I thought to be a hospital ward. There were many rows of beds very close to one another with a table alongside each. A score of lights shone down from the ceiling. Middle-aged women in tweed costumes were bustling around with plates. I watched one of them come up to me and put a plate on the table.

"There you are," she said. "A nice plate of stew. You'll feel better after you've eaten something."

This seemed to be a most uncomfortable, noisy and over-crowded place. I felt disappointed. I wanted to escape to a room of my own where I could sleep in peace.

Presently the woman in tweeds returned.

"Why don't you start?" she asked. "You're letting your stew get cold."

Even if I had been able to control my limbs the last thing I wanted to do was to eat.

She persisted: "I'll help you." She fussed round me trying to sit me up.

A man walked by.

"Oh, Doctor!" she called. "He isn't eating his stew."

The doctor came up and looked at me:

"Don't trouble," he said, "he's beyond it. We'll get him away quickly."

I remember my feeling of relief when I found myself being carried on a stretcher through the darkness and then put into an ambulance. I do not recall whether or not there was a nurse in there with me.

Next came a series of vague impressions.

The interior of the dark ambulance and the purr of wheels moving along a smooth road.

Being pushed along a lighted passage on a trolley.

A man doing something around my head. He seemed to be cutting my hair.

10

No Memorial

A tall figure in a white overall bending over me with a syringe and saying:

"Just a little prick and then you'll fall asleep immediately."

I felt the prick. There was a gentle, pleasant humming in my ears. 'This,' I thought, 'is the end of the battle.' Others were taking over. I could now cease to struggle and relax.

A wave of sleep swept over my body, starting with my legs, creeping up, and in a few seconds enveloping my brain.

CHAPTER II

FOR a time I was swimming under water, trying desperately hard to reach the surface. I could feel the pressure on top of me; a heaviness in my head and my ears, and a throbbing silence. I struggled for air; I twisted and kicked.

Then the pressure was easing. Suddenly I broke the surface.

There were faces peering down at me and someone was saying:

"Wake up! You've been sleeping long enough. You must wake up."

I opened my eyes wide. The room was full of nurses, and a doctor was taking my pulse. He looked at me and smiled.

"It's all over now," he said. "It was a wonderful operation. We got all the shrapnel out of your head. You will find you're unable to talk and unable to move your right arm or right leg at all, but don't think about that yet; we know all about it."

I felt tired and weak. I wanted to sleep for days and months before I started to concentrate again on being alive. So I closed my eyes and almost at once I fell asleep.

The next time I woke up there were two young nurses by my bed. My head seemed to be laced in bandages some of which were joined under my chin. The room was extremely bare and had a brown linoleum floor; there was one large brown cupboard and a bedside locker. The black-out boards were in position and the room was lighted by an unshaded, hanging electric bulb.

One of the V.A.D.s shook a thermometer and pushed it under my tongue. I could not feel anything, and I heard the glass casing snap. When this happened both the nurses became excited. They removed the broken ends and

12

started to dab the inside of my mouth with lumps of cotton-wool.

"You must never tell Sister about this," one of them said. But I was not the slightest bit interested; I felt sleepy again and I only wanted to be left alone.

During that night I woke up a number of times.

Once one of the surgeons who had operated on my head came to see me. He was a small man with grey hair and a pleasant face.

"I wonder," he said to the nurse, "if he is any relation to a family I knew in Ireland? Tobias is an unusual name."

He turned to me. "Are you connected with ——?" He mentioned a relative of mine.

I attempted to nod affirmatively and found myself shaking my head negatively.

A young Sister came in and spoke to the surgeon in a whisper. I caught her words.

"He came in with no papers," she said, "so we have been unable to notify his next-of-kin."

The surgeon spoke to me again.

"Do you think you could write down your home address?"

I felt certain I could manage it. My brain was quite clear and I knew what I wished to write.

The Sister held a writing block for me and the surgeon put a pencil in my left hand.

I started to write, but to my surprise I merely drew a series of very crooked lines. I tried again, with the same result. I seemed completely unable to transmit directions from my brain to my hand. I wanted to go on trying, but the surgeon removed the pencil.

"It's no use," he said. "He can't do it. They'll probably send the information later."

Usually when I woke up there was a rubber tube round my arm and a nurse or Sister was sitting by my bed taking almost continual readings of my blood pressure. The

13

doctor who had spoken to me when I first came round was often there too, feeling my pulse and asking me to follow his finger with my eyes as he moved it around in front of me.

The night seemed endless. It was impossible to gauge the passage of time by the changing light outside the windows, for the black-out boards were never removed. I think my periods of sleep or unconsciousness must have been very short. Afterwards, I was able to remember at least a dozen different occasions when I was awake and there were probably a lot more.

At last when I awoke out of what seemed a somewhat longer sleep it was broad daylight. A nurse with dark curly hair and an attractive, smiling face was dusting my bedside locker. When she saw me watching her she continued her work but started talking to me.

"They call me Boxing Day!" she said. "Isn't it silly? They have nicknames for all the nurses—no respect at all. I suppose that's because we're only V.A.D.s and not proper nurses. But we call the patients by special names too. Never 'Sir' like we're supposed to."

She chattered on happily and I enjoyed her bright company.

"I wonder what we'll call you? Tobias—Tobias," she repeated thoughtfully. "I know! I've got it! Of course, we'll christen you 'Toby'. I'll tell everyone."

Later she returned with another V.A.D. A plump blonde whom 'Boxing Day' introduced as 'Fido'. Together they fed me; literally fed me as I was lying motionless on my back and they transferred food from a plate into my mouth. Then they made me drink out of a cup with a long, narrow spout; this was extraordinarily difficult as too much fluid used to pour out and almost choke me.

As the day wore on I received countless visits from doctors, Sisters and nurses. The V.A.D.s seemed to be all pretty, vivacious, and eager to help. Each introduced herself by her nickname when she first entered. There

14

were 'Sunshine', 'Butterfly', 'Goldie-Locks', 'Fluffy', and many more. They all called me 'Toby'.

I slept most of the time, waking up for meals, toilet necessities, injections, pills and washing.

An Army barber came to shave me. It was an odd experience as my face seemed to be divided by a line drawn exactly down the centre. On the left side of the demarcation I could feel normal sensations, but on the right side I had no feeling at all.

During the late afternoon I took a turn for the worse. The blood-pressure instrument was re-connected to my arm and a nurse sat by my side. I felt that what strength I had left was slowly ebbing away. Everything seemed far distant and my impressions were gradually becoming blurred.

Then an unshakable idea came into my mind that I must stay awake at all costs, because if I did not I would die. For a long time I struggled using all the mental energy I could muster. In the end I drifted off to sleep.

That evening all the V.A.D.s tiptoed in to say good-night and one of the night staff, whom they called 'Dozey', took up the vigil at my bedside.

All that night 'Dozey' and another nurse took it in turns to sit with me. The overhead light was turned off and a pale green night-lamp was brought in. I slept intermittently, but there seemed to be so many interruptions: routine inspections by doctors and the usual pills and injections.

The Night Sister, a big girl whom I could imagine a hockey centre-forward, made an omelette for me as I was not able to eat the supper they had brought round. She sat on my bed for a while after I had finished.

"You'll be through the worst in a day or two," she told me. "You have an awfully powerful constitution which will see you out of danger."

As it turned out, three more days and three more nights passed by without much change in my condition. My memories of that time are hazy. Eventually they gave up

15

staying with me all the time and pinned a bell-push on the blanket beside my left hand. Even if I did not ring I was never left alone for long periods.

The V.A.D.s were marvellous at understanding my feeble sign-language and invariably, without any bother, they grasped what I wanted the moment I started to gesticulate. If I cupped my hand and raised it to my mouth they would produce a drink, and when my head was torn with an acute headache I would clap my hand on my forehead and they would hurry off to fetch some tablets.

On the fifth morning I felt better. I was woken early by the Night Sister for a wash, as she always liked to wash me herself.

I tried to smile at her and she seemed pleased.

"Well, that's better! You look a different man to-day. You'll become stronger all the time from now on."

I had not noticed before that I had blankets over and under me without sheets. Also, I was lying in bed naked. Vaguely I wondered why.

When the Sister had finished, she squatted on the bed and placed her hand across my forehead.

"Listen, Toby," she said. "You have got to be very patient. You have a long, difficult spell ahead of you. Your soldiering days are over now. If you really make an effort you will get some movement back in your arm and leg; but you ought to know this, they think you may never be able to talk again. Make up your mind that it's not going to get you down; after all, your eyes are far more important than your voice."

When she had gone the realisation of my condition came to me. I was lying on my back almost unable to move in my bed—and I was completely dumb. Slowly the full significance of my plight sank in; they thought I would never speak again and there was only a possibility of my ever being able to use one leg and one arm. But the whole thing was unthinkable! It could not really be me this was happening to. I had always been so fit.

16

Was it all an unpleasant dream? I closed my eyes and tried to place my hands above my head; the left arm responded—but my right arm was no longer my own. And yet it was all too vivid and realistic to be a dream. And in any case I did not possess the imaginative powers to create so fantastic a situation.

All day I thought of the Sister's words, and I began to realise that even if the very worst happened and I was to be a dumb, helpless invalid for the remainder of my life, my whole being, in spite of that, was spurred by a passionate desire to live. There must still be something left; some motive, some happiness, some fulfilment.

And yet so much was finished for ever. So much that had mattered such a lot. The fragmentary ecstasies of sport; the split second when the ball is in your hands and the kaleidoscope of coloured shirts shifts suddenly leaving a scant opening in front of you; the smell of mud, and the corner-flag, and the frenzied crowds on the touchline. The even creak of oars in the rowlocks and the other crew seen out of the corner of your eye through a flurry of spray as your boat is creeping up on theirs.

Sport also produced its moments of tranquillity. The ease and pace of the bath tub after the match; hot water, soap, and a feeling of delicious languor. Summer evenings on river banks with the last 'Finals' still being rowed and a regatta band playing in half-light.

Life had been scintillating, effervescent, and full of certainties. I had been strong, confident, and impregnable.

Of course there were other things; things which had been stored away to be examined when there was more time. For instance, that uncontrollable surging in the breast at a symphony concert or that exalted joyousness when reading a favourite poem. Those seemed likely to be the gratifications of middle age.

But the tempo of living had never slackened. Every moment had been thrilling and wonderful because I had been young, blessed, and privileged. Nothing had ever

17

been wasted; there was even something vital about those memories of smiling made-up faces, seen through a haze of tobacco smoke, while in the background the tinkle of glasses mingled with the deliberate, thumped tunes which were being ground out of an ill-tuned piano.

Nothing had been wasted in the past and I could look back on my life without any regrets. That life was now irretrievably ended. I was dead, and I had been born again —at any rate physically. But deep inside of me there was an indefinable essential that continued from my first existence into my second; there was something apart from the realities of living; some spirit, personality, or soul which circled above, able to perceive the river both before the bend and after it as well.

Nothing could destroy my faith in the future. It was a blind, unreasoning faith which burned within me with an unquenchable fire. Perhaps, unknown to me, it was the spiritual impetus of Christianity. Religion, however, had been one of the vast subjects which I had laid aside to be studied later on when the years had blunted the eager vitality of my youth.

I soon found out that if I was to recover in any way completely my active co-operation was to be essential. The natural healing process would carry me a certain way, but beyond that the distance I travelled would be dependent on my own effort. This was told to me by the chief physiotherapist, who came to see me one morning a few weeks after my operation.

"You will have daily massage," she said. "Nobody can tell how much nerve damage your arm and leg have suffered. You'll have to concentrate on getting the maximum movement back which is possible in the circumstances."

That same morning a little lady in Red Cross uniform visited me. She sat down beside me and started to introduce herself, shyly and half apologetically.

"I'm the speech therapist," she said. "I'm going to teach you to speak again."

18

She told me that she did not want me to look on her lessons as a hill which I had already climbed in my infancy, but she wished me to regard them as a new and interesting study. Everybody took speech for granted, she said, they never analysed the formation of sounds and syllables. Gradually, as she warmed to her subject, she lost her shyness. I watched her fascinated. She was so small and yet her presence filled the room; she was as frail as a delicate little china ornament and yet she exuded strength; her voice was quiet and bell-like and yet she was magnetic and forceful in everything she said.

"At present," she went on, "you will not be able to make any sounds at all, so I will come to see you each day and merely talk to you about anything that comes into my head. Later on, when you begin to make sounds, we will really get down to it. Meanwhile, in all your thoughts never visualise a future in which you are unable to speak. Between us I am certain we will get back your voice."

As I started to feel better in myself my loss of speech began to trouble me more. I felt the loneliness most of all; the inability to hold even the shortest conversation. There was a sense of frustration too; sometimes when I wished to communicate the most simple requirements to a nurse it would end after countless false trails and irrelevant guesses in a hopeless impasse—like two strangers speaking in different tongues. I tried not to worry over the awful abstract implication of dumbness, but every now and then my thoughts burst out from the flimsy barriers of self-discipline and a blackness rose up before me and there was an endless falling away in my stomach. Physical fears are infinitely preferable to the terrors of the mind.

I was not certain how much I would be incapacitated if my right side remained completely paralysed. At the worst, I supposed, I might be permanently confined to my bed, or perhaps I might achieve a certain amount of independence in a wheel-chair. The idea of being completely dependent on others was the most depressing of all my

19

visions of the future. Even now in my present condition I was beginning to find it irksome.

I knew that I would have to find some way to combat the long, restless hours of mental inactivity. I tried to signal to a nurse that I would like to see a newspaper. At length she understood and brought one to me. I held it up and looked at the headlines; I found that I could see the letters quite clearly, yet I could not understand them; they might have been Chinese characters, for all they meant to me. Obviously, for the present, I was not able to read.

I started a process of reasoning. If I was to get better I wanted something to which I could look forward; something to be achieved, so that, if everything else in my life was to be cast aside on the rubbish-heap of 'might-have-beens', this, at any rate, would be an objective to which I would devote all my remaining powers. It must be something which I could still do even if I was never again able to speak or to leave my bed.

After hours of thought I conceived an idea. I would learn to write with my left hand and I would write a novel. In the meanwhile, so long as I remained very ill, I would concentrate on the plot, so that when the time came and I was able to begin setting pen to paper I would know in detail my situations, my characters, and the whole structure of the story.

And so, day after day, I lay on my back endlessly constructing, modifying and correcting, until the little puppet world inside my mind became almost as real for me as the circumscribed life in which I was actually taking part.

I always enjoyed the visits of Miss Heywood, the speech therapist. Both when she was speaking to me and in her moments of silence she inspired me with immense hopefulness. I also looked forward to my daily session with the young assistant physiotherapist who had been put in charge of my case; she was good company in spite of her obvious difficulty in keeping up a bright, one-sided conversation

20

with a man about whose views and interests she knew absolutely nothing.

At the end of three weeks my leg had recovered a little sensitivity and a slight, very feeble movement, but my arm and shoulder remained depressingly lifeless.

One morning when Boxing Day was dusting my room she said:

"We've got a surprise for you this morning, Toby. We're putting you in another room. You're well enough now and the company will do you good. You'll like Kurt, everybody does; he's a Norwegian paratroop captain."

My new room was slightly larger than the old one. One bed, into which they put me, was just inside the door and there was another running parallel to the right, just under the window.

Kurt was tall, broad, blonde, and immensely handsome. He was up for most of the day and walked about in battle-dress. He sat on my bed as soon as the change-over was completed.

"I will look after you," he said, speaking with a charming Norwegian accent. "Anything you want—I get to know your signals. Later, I teach you to talk. Try now—One, two, three—one, two, three," he repeated slowly.

I tried to follow, but no sound emerged from my mouth. He shook his head sadly.

"No. Not yet. Later on. We try a little every day."

The hospital authorities had managed to contact my family, who immediately came down to see me. It was a most trying experience for everybody. They had not been given any details about my condition but told simply that I had been wounded in the head. When they had recovered from the shock of realising that I could not speak there followed half an hour of agonising attempts at conversation with words on their side and gestures on mine. Eventually Kurt came in and rendered what assistance he could.

My leg started to improve almost noticeably each day. This encouraged me a good deal. Each morning when I

21

woke up I was almost afraid to try to move my arm or to speak, because I knew that if I could get no response I would have to wait another twenty-four hours for a renewal of hope.

Miss Heywood gradually became the symbol of all my expectations and my faith; she seemed to be possessed of some magical power, some key that would unlatch the staunchest locks. As I was stumbling and groping my way through the entrance of the tunnel she was tranquil and confident, as though she had traversed it many times before and she knew that it would lead eventually from darkness into light.

"It's taking a long time," she said on one occasion, "but it will come; in God's good time it will surely come."

CHAPTER III

ONE day the physiotherapist suggested I might like to start learning a form of deaf-and-dumb alphabet. I shook my head in vigorous protestation; that would be too much like a final abandonment of hope. I had begun to notice a slight change in the attitude of the staff towards me. They no longer came in every morning to try to make me talk: they had even given up reassuring me quite so emphatically that I would recover my power of speech. I seemed to sense a slight uneasiness when they were with me, the lack of ease of an honest person who is being forced to deceive.

Only Kurt and Miss Heywood remained the same. Kurt persevered absolutely tirelessly.

"One, two, three. Say that slowly after me. One, two, three."

Kurt was with me when it happened.

I made a gigantic, supreme effort to copy him, exerting my entire mental and physical strength. The sound which I emitted was a choking, distorted parody of speech.

Kurt looked at me, amazed and unbelieving.

"Do that again," he commanded.

I obeyed.

Suddenly he sprang from his chair:

"You talked!" he shouted. "You talked!"

He rushed out of the room yelling at the top of his voice:

"Toby's talking. I have taught him. Toby's talking."

Presently the Sister and half-a-dozen V.A.D.s were grouped around my bed.

Kurt stood there proudly like an inventor demonstrating his latest device.

"Now, I show," he said. "Right, Toby. Say after me: One, two, three."

23

I let out my new sound and at once everybody began to clamour excitedly.

"Quiet, girls," Kurt said. "Now, again, Toby."

"No," said Sister firmly. "Not again. You don't want to tire him out. Now, back to work, nurses." She scattered them playfully with her hands. Then she turned to me.

"Good show, Toby. That's a start at any rate. But don't expect anything spectacular; it will be years before you can speak anything like normally. Just keep on doing what Miss Heywood tells you—and for goodness sake don't start speaking with a Norwegian accent!"

Miss Heywood received the news calmly but with evident delight.

"Now we can start speech exercises," she said. For half an hour she made various vocal sounds and I endeavoured to follow her.

My voice did not improve quickly. I was soon able to gabble as unintelligibly as a one-year-old baby, but I still had to rely for the main part on hand-made signals when I wanted anything.

Several people from other wards started visiting me. I appreciated their friendliness and realised how difficult they must find it to converse with one who could not speak. A middle-aged man in a shabby dressing-gown used to come in every afternoon and ask how I was getting on. Kurt told me that he was a general who had once been Governor of Gibraltar. "He calls on every officer here each day for a chat," said Kurt. "He's a fine man. He calls people by their christian names always."

I was still feeling very weak and unbalanced when they first sat me up in a chair. After five minutes I could sustain the effort no longer, so I rang my bell and signified I wanted to be put back to bed. During the following days I became more sure of myself and I even started looking forward to my brief outing.

There was absolutely no sign of life in my right arm

and shoulder, but my leg was responding well to treatment.

The weather had become intensely cold; snow caked across the windows and piled up on the ledges.

"We are better off in here at present," said Kurt. "I leave in time for the spring offensive when it is sunshine again."

He had numerous girl-friends both among the V.A.D.s and in the neighbouring town. He used to tell me about them when he had returned from one of his many engagements.

"I had lunch with Diana. Quite nice but she talks very much."

I soon realised that women completely spoilt him. They were all captivated by his exceptional good looks and his charming manners.

One morning he walked in with the Sister. They both came to my bed.

"Toby," said Kurt, "I am once more fit. I am discharged to-morrow."

"I'm afraid it's true," added Sister. "We hung on to him as long as we possibly could. Now, Toby, the problem is what we're going to do with you. I think, personally, when Kurt goes you'd be far better off in the big ward. There's plenty of company there and you'd get lots of chances to practise talking."

I had some idea how unpleasant a big ward might be, but I also knew how lonely one can be in a single or a double room.

The main officers' surgical ward at the hospital was a large, bright room with about a dozen beds ranged round the walls. Usually patients were put into side wards when they first came in, and eventually graduated to it when another intake of fresh cases was admitted and when they themselves were no longer critically ill. The hospital only dealt with serious head and spinal injuries, so that people usually remained for a considerable length of time.

It is one of the characteristics of ward life that when you

have been a member of any ward for three days you might well have been there for a score of years. At first, being unable to take part in conversation, I passed the time by studying the interplay of the various personalities around me. I intended to remain a mere onlooker observing what took place from a seat apart, but I found myself drawn reluctantly into the arena and submerged by the narrow atmosphere inside the four walls which imprisoned us. I hated it all from the start. I hated the lack of privacy, the crude parochial humour, the cynicism and bitterness, and the forced joviality which interspersed those awful black hours of depression, and the wireless continuously blaring the latest jazz favourites. I was constantly aware that every one of us was enacting a terrible climax in his life, fighting a lonely battle against an invisible power whose aims were a sad mockery of love and reason; but instead of drama, courage, and nobility I could only witness the days slowly dragging past, each one as aimless, as empty, and as futile as the last.

When my mind travels back to those times I see people rather than events. The routine happenings have become dissipated in the ephemeral pools of memory, but the individuals around whom they took place stand out vividly in face, mannerism, and character.

There was 'Fitch', a Pole, who had lost an eye at Arnhem. He knew that Poland's fate was at the mercy of geographical chance and her only immediate 'liberation' would be the mere substitution of a Russian tyranny for the closing epoch of insane German brutality. But Fitch had much more than this to worry about. He was convinced that he was losing the sight of his single remaining eye. For hours he used to lie on his bed, silent and staring. Perhaps he found it difficult at such a moment to be in an alien land surrounded by strangers; strangers who, however polite and obliging, did not operate on his own wavelength.

The most pathetic man in the ward was Dick Brumley. The screens were nearly always around his bed as he required a lot of treatment. I think he was usually in pain although he never complained. Dick had been wounded in the spine and he was paralysed from the waist down. He thought he was going to get well, but we all knew through that strange system of hospital bush telepathy that he would never leave his bed again.

When I first arrived Dick's wife and baby were staying in the town. Eventually he sent her back to look after his shop in the Midlands, telling her that she should come down again when he was better so that she could wheel him out in a chair.

After they had told Dick that he would never walk again he was silent for three whole days—so were the rest of us. Then one morning they fetched him suddenly and moved him to another hospital nearer his Birmingham home.

I immediately took a liking to Dermot O'Malley, who had broken his back when serving with an Irish cavalry regiment in Normandy. His mother used to take him out every afternoon in a spinal carriage; usually she was escorted by a bevy of beautiful girls, for Dermot was very charming, very handsome, very young and very gay.

Another bright personality was Peter Livingstone, a Mosquito pilot. He had just completed a hazardous and successful tour of night-flying operations when he had broken his neck vaulting over a chair in a Mess rag. Peter had endured a long spell in bed, but when I first knew him he was walking around in a plaster jacket and wearing a leather collar round his neck. He used to go out like this nearly every evening to public-houses and dance-halls.

I was put at first into a corner bed beside a window. As I looked out at the other patients hobbling round the gardens I used to think: 'If only I could stumble about out there I would ask for nothing more.'

My immediate neighbour was a Welshman, Captain Rees, whose brain had been affected by a dreadful head wound. He never spoke much, and his wife, who was with

27

him most afternoons and evenings, had an unenviable time looking after him. He liked to tease. Once when it was snowing he opened the window over my bed so that the wind and snow blew all over me; then he stood back rocking with laughter. My bed was in three sections, each elevated and depressed by a lever at the foot. A favourite game of his was to raise the top and bottom sections, to my chronic discomfort. When this happened the others used to ring for a nurse, who would restrain him and set me right again.

I suppose I should have been flattered by his rather odd attentions, because he ignored everybody else in the ward. There was something tragically childlike about him. Once the Sister came in to see me. Quite incidentally she remarked that she had been reading my papers and had noticed that I had been wounded on a previous occasion. That evening the Welshman asked his wife to sew an additional wound-stripe on his tunic beside the one he usually wore. She protestingly did so, and he came over to me flaunting the two gold bars on his sleeve.

"You see," he said delightedly, "you're not the only one around here who's been wounded twice."

One day he showed me a photograph of himself as he had been. The contrast was so sad I had to look away.

My memory recalls other people. The Eighth Army padre who was always joking about his disfigured face.

"My chances of marriage are now pretty meagre," he used to say.

There was the Royal Armoured Corps lieutenant, more lightly wounded than the rest of us, who was terrified of being sent back to fight. He did not mention his fears during the daytime, but jabbered about them incessantly when he was asleep.

And the rich young officer from the Brigade of Guards who was paralysed, bitter, and bewildered. A short while previously his life had been full and promising. He had been an athlete and a scholar and a darling of society. Then

28

a sniper's bullet had completely shattered everything for which he lived.

And the two 'civilians' who had been invalided out of the Army during their treatment. Perhaps it was this common bond which drew them together in a close friendship, broken intermittently by fierce rows. Ralph was an agricultural student, wounded a long time back at El Alamein. George was a prospective civil engineer who had been blown up on a mine at Cassino and was always going up to the operating theatre to have more fragments of metal removed from various parts of his body.

Many came and many went while I was in my corner bed. But the war was drawing to an end by that time. Somebody once said we were the backwash of a glorious victory. That was a particularly cynical remark; and yet I have often thought how instructive it would have been for anybody who was still foolish enough to retain any illusions about the manifold glories of battle to have spent a month or two in that ward looking out over the wreckage of so many youthful lives.

CHAPTER IV

ONE day the sensation began to return to my right arm and shoulder; then I found I could move them about feebly and slowly.

The doctor who was looking after me tested my new movements.

"I'm afraid your arm will always be almost useless," he said. "But your leg is doing fine and might be pretty strong eventually. About your speech——" he hesitated. "You'll be able to take a limited part in conversations after a long course of treatment, but nothing more than that—ever."

It still seemed inconceivable to me that I was to be permanently disabled. At times I simply did not believe it; at others the full truth was apparent and despair ran her frozen fingers over my whole being. It was easier to control one's thoughts in the daytime. At night, however, when the lights were turned out courage waned and reality, grotesque and silent, strutted about the ward.

I used to dream, and in my dreams I was normal and happy. Then I would awaken immediately aware that I had known normality for the last time; I was disabled; I was an invalid. Nothing would be the same again. Life from this on would be a long continuous struggle against heavy odds; a sustained effort to smile and to make-believe when one could no longer enjoy any of the things that mattered most of all.

People discussed endlessly what they were going to do with themselves when they left the Service. There was one thing they all agreed, that no matter how badly one was incapacitated by wounds the scale of pensions was so grossly inadequate that it was absolutely essential to earn some sort of income in order to exist at all. This talk filled me with depression. So did the stories about the large firms who deliberately found charitable openings for the

30

disabled and employed them, like so many passengers, in compassionate gratitude for their unfortunate war records. It seemed to be everybody's ambition to find such an opening. The thought made me shudder. To so resign oneself; to adopt the insignia and label of a permanent crock. One golden truth shone out in my mind: that one must get back to normality; that wounds must not make any difference; they must be accepted as a challenge and, so far as possible, they must be overcome. To me it did not seem to be a courageous thought so much as a selfish desire not to be excluded from life. For the same reason a soldier who is crippled with weariness still drags himself along after the retreating columns of his comrades rather than give way to his exhaustion and fall into the hands of the enemy.

Before I had joined the Army I had taken a preliminary step towards becoming a barrister. My papers described me even now as a student at the Inns of Court. Wisdom demanded that I should erase that type of career from my thoughts. I had suffered a brain wound; I was almost dumb; I had in no way committed myself except to proclaim my choice of a career. And yet I became obsessed with the thought that I must keep on. Even if all the rest allowed themselves to be defeated I must still adhere to the way of life I had chosen for myself. I saw the whole thing as a personal battle against fate. I knew that if I resigned myself to the obvious I would spend all my future years in bitterness and regret, but that if I persisted and qualified as a barrister, whatever additional blows destiny might strike me in the future I would still have the tremendous individual satisfaction of knowing that her first onslaught had not battered me into surrender.

I did not tell anybody what I was thinking, but I made a secret vow that I would dedicate myself entirely during the immediately succeeding years towards qualifying, even as I would have done if I had been lucky enough to come through the war unscathed.

Immediately I began to feel more contented. I now had some aim in the future to which I could cling; some destination towards which I could travel. It was senseless to look too far ahead; it was better to progress from one limited objective to another; to climb from one hill to the next without casting any longing glances upwards at the crest of the mountain.

I decided to carry out an experiment. It was to tap the only possible source of strength that could aid me in my struggle. I made up my mind to pray to God regularly and consistently for His assistance in my new scheme of life. I had my doubts about the efficacy of prayer; but it was worth trying; anything was worth trying. Even if God did exist and even if the Bible teaching were true, it was clear that Divine aid would be granted more readily to the weak and afflicted than to the strong and ambitious; prayer was not intended so that a king might seek more glory; rather, for the wandering beggar to find shelter from the storm.

I tried to say the Lord's Prayer. But when my brain started to draw forth the oft-repeated words it stuttered and failed like a powerless, broken machine. My mind went completely blank. I realised then how difficult it was going to be to fulfil my plan.

Miss Heywood's lessons were becoming longer. She was very firm; no matter if I did not feel well, no matter if I had a severe headache, the speech exercise must go on. She also used to read to me in order to improve my concentration. The book she had chosen was a thriller by Agatha Christie. I only half listened, but the rest of the ward followed the story with avid interest and when Miss Heywood produced the book from her brief-case there used to be a general move towards my bed of everyone who was fit to walk about.

Winter had ended and spring, pure, fresh, and hopeful, was at hand. I could see yellow and purple crocuses from my window and the trees in the garden seemed green and full of vitality. I think it affected us all and a new spirit of cheerfulness was apparent in the ward. Boxing Day and some of the other V.A.D.s promised to take me out in a chair as soon as the doctor would grant his permission. I seemed suddenly to be making real progress.

Then one night I felt an intense pain in my chest. I reported it and I was X-rayed. The Sister told me the result.

"Unfortunately," she said, "you have pleurisy on your paralysed side." She then told me I would have to stay in bed until it cleared up.

After a week the pain had vanished and I was allowed to resume sitting out and practising walking short distances. The muscles in my leg and foot were still very weak and I had to use a toe-spring, a contraption which kept your foot supported at right-angles to your leg.

I was delighted when the brigadier in charge of the hospital told me I could go away for a month.

"You have still a hard and tedious time ahead of you," he remarked. "But I think a change would do you all the good in the world."

He told me I would have to have another operation. They intended to open my scalp and to graft a tantalum plate into my skull to fill up the cavity there.

My doctor suggested a few weeks at the seaside, so I arranged to go with my mother to a hotel on the South Coast near to the port where my younger sister was stationed in the W.R.N.S. I was feeling increasingly independent now, as I could hobble around leaning on a stick.

One of the many excellent jobs the ladies of the Women's Voluntary Service were doing at this time was driving the wounded around the country in private cars. This long-distance taxi service, for which they would accept no payment, was carried out with a competency and kindness which made us all very grateful.

It was thrilling after so many months in hospital to be driven along the sunlit, country lanes and to see people—normal, fit people—going about their daily lives.

We stopped once at a wayside hotel, where we had lunch. I remember wishing others would not stare so much, although their interest was obviously sympathetic and I must have looked very conspicuous with my stick, my arm hanging useless, and my bandaged head.

The hotel where we were going to stay was on the sea front and seemed a pleasant place. The staff went out of their way from the start to look after me. In particular there was a head waiter who had served in France during the First World War, and loved to talk to me about the torn and weary towns of the Somme; he tenderly enquired, as a man might ask after the long-lost loves of his youth, about Amiens, Arras, and Neuve-Chapelle.

Every morning my mother and I used to walk along the sea-wall and afterwards, sometimes, we would go into the town for a cup of coffee.

About this time I tried to read a book. It proved a laborious business. I could only take in the words very slowly, and in addition whenever I came to the end of a line and flicked my eyes back to the start of the next, normally such an involuntary movement, I became lost and started to read a wrong line. Writing was even more discouraging. It was awkward enough to hold a pen in my left hand, but a thing I found even more troublesome was the fact that I had entirely lost the art of spelling—even ridiculously simple words. I did not seem capable of visualising them on paper at all.

At this hotel I met, for the first time, a type of person whom I was to encounter fairly frequently during the next few years. He came up to me in the lounge and enquired the nature of my injury. I told him and then he started his own story:

"I was just like that," nodding at my arm (they had always had exactly the same trouble as oneself). He held up his own arm and surveyed it sadly.

"It was in the middle of a rugger match. I thought I

would never get the use of it again—but——" he paused and smiled self-indulgently, "I was determined to get better and now, look!"—suddenly his inanimate hand was galvanised into life; every joint and muscle seemed to be moving furiously at the same time; it reminded me of the frenzied struggles of an upturned beetle.

At the end of the month I felt considerably stronger. I had discarded my toe-spring and although I still limped I could walk considerable distances using a stick. I had stopped wearing a bandage round my head too and the hair had grown long enough to partially hide the dent and the scar.

CHAPTER V

BOXING DAY met me in a taxi at the station on my return to hospital.

"To-night we're going to a dance," she said.

"I hope you enjoy it," I replied.

"I hope *we* enjoy it," she laughed. "You're coming too, Toby; five V.A.D.s and five patients."

"But that's ridiculous——" I began.

She cut me short.

"You're coming, and that's the end of it. You're taking me."

I was given a bed in the old ward surrounded by a lot of new faces, but several old ones as well, including Flight-Lieutenant Peter Livingstone still in a leather collar, and Lieutenant Dermot O'Malley, who had returned from leave that same day.

These two were both in the party that evening. It was a weekly dance held at the local Officers' Club and a special invitation had been issued to the patients at our hospital to send along all those who were well enough to attend.

We were received by the lady organiser, who immediately separated us from our V.A.D.s and handed each of us over to one of her hostesses. Mine was a pretty little blonde who plainly looked upon the whole affair as a rather boring and tedious duty.

When the band started to play we were sitting by the dance-floor. She regarded me doubtfully.

"Are you legs or arms?" she asked.

"One leg and one arm," I answered.

"Oh, that's difficult, isn't it? You wouldn't be able to dance."

"It would be difficult," I agreed. "But if you'd like to try, I'm willing."

36

"Perhaps not," she said quickly. "How about a drink?"

"I'm not allowed to drink alcohol," I said. "But let's go down to the bar; I can probably get a lemonade or something."

"There may be a bit of a scrum," she said. "Perhaps we'd better not go. We'll stay and talk," she added lamely, "if you don't find it tiring to talk."

I told her I did not. Her eyes were wandering round at the dancing figures and one elegant little foot was beating time to the music. Suddenly her eyes lit up.

"Who's that tall major standing by himself over there?"

I told her he was one of our patients who had been only slightly wounded and was now completely recovered. I offered to introduce him to her.

"Oh no," she said regretfully, "I'm supposed to stay with you."

But I could not see her suffer any longer. I called him over and asked him to give her a dance. I saw her again later in the evening still dancing with him and gazing up dreamily into his eyes.

I continued to sit alone, feeling unwanted and depressed. 'I'm simply an old crock,' I thought. 'I'm only in the way here. I will never go to dances again.'

"Have you lost little Blondie?" Boxing Day laughed as she sat down beside me. "I thought you wouldn't be quite her cup of tea. Anyhow, I'm glad she's gone as I'm going to show you that you can still dance after a fashion."

She devoted the remainder of the evening to me and we went round and round the floor. She was continually pushed, bumped, kicked and trodden on, but I think she enjoyed herself almost as much as I did myself.

A few days later the brigadier of the hospital did one of his rounds. He inspected my head and looked at my notes.

"I'm afraid you're not ready for your operation yet," he said. "I think we'll send you for a couple of months to the convalescent home at Lowther Hall in Sussex. Meanwhile you can leave the ward and move into a room upstairs—it's more comfortable there."

Dermot O'Malley was also transferred upstairs. He and I endeavoured to get a room together as they all held two people, but the Sister had arranged differently as she liked to have the rooms occupied by men of the same rank.

My new companion was an amazing personality, David Brewster. David was at the War Office and had some sort of job connected with the designing and testing of personal equipment. He had sustained some damage to his spine on a field exercise, though the doctors were not certain what was the nature of the trouble. At that time he was merely under observation. He had an embarrassing respect for those of us who had been wounded in action and harboured the astounding belief that there was something rather ignominious about the way he had received his own injury.

There were quite a number of patients hanging around rather aimlessly waiting for transfers, operations or medical boards. The hospital provided no amenities except a small, sparsely furnished sitting-room, so we all spent most of our time in the town. David, Dermot and I each had friends living round about, so we pooled our resources and found as a consequence that few days were devoid of some entertainment. We often spent an afternoon at the cinema, an evening at the theatre, or dining at a hotel and afterwards adjourning to the bar. Of course these two, being spinal cases, had had no limitations imposed on their consumption of alcohol, and I found it difficult to travel by myself through their various moods of jollity and abandonment on the strength of a couple of glasses of orange juice. I must have been dull company, but they tolerated me.

I had ceased to be so worried about the future. I was perfectly mobile, and my speech, however stumbling and hesitant, was sufficient for conversation with people who knew me and who would listen patiently. I was gaining confidence that things would somehow work themselves

out satisfactorily. However, there were occasional reminders that it was too early for complacency. One
morning I was dawdling over my breakfast. The man
sitting opposite asked suddenly:

"Have you had many fits so far?"

"Fits?" I looked at him blankly.

"Don't tell me you don't know about it," he said. "We
all get them. Once you've had a brain injury you go on
having fits periodically for the rest of your life. I have one
every three weeks."

I left the table immediately and went to the room in
which my doctor did his office work. He called me in and
made me sit down.

"Well, Toby. What is it?" he asked, pushing aside his
papers.

"Fits," I replied.

"Ah, yes—fits."

"We all get them, Doc. Don't we?"

"Well—nearly all of you."

"What about me?"

"Quite frankly, it's most probable from the position and
nature of your wound. I'm rather surprised you've got
away with it so far."

"But that means I'm finished from a point of view of a
career?"

He shrugged. "Of course it doesn't cause hereditary
epilepsy, only a traumatic one."

"Is there any hope of getting clear without them?"

"There's always hope in medical science. If two years
pass since your wound and you haven't had a fit you can
be relatively confident. If five years pass without one
you'll be absolutely safe and immune. That's why you'll
have to go on taking luminal for five years, even if nothing
happens, to keep your brain damped down."

After that I had to go for my daily lesson with Miss
Heywood. I saw her in her own room now and I had
progressed as far as being able to read a book out loud.

At every mistake I made she used to insist that I re-read the whole passage. At the end of the lesson I asked her bluntly if my voice would ever be good enough to permit me to practise as a barrister.

"I'll tell you that before you're discharged from hospital. Of course it will only be my own opinion and I'm not a doctor."

"I wonder if I'm just kidding myself about the future," I remarked. "It's rather like planning a fool's paradise to hope to pass exams with a damped-down brain and periodic fits."

She looked at me for a moment and then said firmly:

"You must never give way to thoughts like those. Courage and faith can overcome many disadvantages, and the things for which you have to struggle really hard are always the most worth while."

We were all suffering at that stage from an 'ungrateful country' complex. We used to look out avidly for any words or actions which proved that now that England had finished with our services we were to be treated as so much useless litter and that there was no place for us in the flushed, victorious society of the future. In our imagination humanity had already raised its elbows against us; sneers and callousness were to be our lot for ever after. The fact that we felt ourselves as aliens in a hostile crowd strengthened the bonds of friendship amongst us.

The two 'civilians', Ralph and George, told us one evening that they had stood for an hour on the roadside unsuccessfully trying to thumb a lift to the town. Empty car after empty car had passed by, and the drivers had ignored their gesticulations—and their crutches.

Day after day men bearing obvious disabilities told how they had been obliged to stand in discomfort in over-crowded buses while the young and the fit had occupied all the seats.

Every one of us had encountered the rudeness and the unhelpfulness which were rife in the country at that time, due largely, though we did not recognise it then, to the fact that so many civilians had been living on their nerves for almost six years and were near to breaking point.

When someone received different treatment a breath of hope stirred through our stagnant spirits. Dermot was offered a seat in a bus by an elderly gentleman; he declined at first owing to the man's age, but the other insisted.

"It is a privilege to do this for you," he said charmingly. "I can see that you've been doing something for me."

Nobody resented this 'ingratitude' more keenly than David. His resentment sometimes caused us acute embarrassment. On one occasion several of us were waiting at a bus stop. When the bus came in and Dermot was about to clamber on board a lady pushed in front of him. Straight away David sprang forward.

"Madam," he exploded, "aren't you ashamed of yourself? Don't you see who these chaps are?" indicating the sticks and bandages.

She went scarlet (I think the rest of us did too) and stood back.

We remonstrated with David and implored him not to repeat this performance again. But only a short while afterwards a similar incident occurred outside a cinema. We had arrived there after lunch, before the place had opened up. A very officious youth in commissionaire's uniform told us that no one would be on duty in the box office for about ten minutes. It was raining hard, so we decided to wait in the vestibule.

"You can't stay in there," said the youth. "You'll have to wait outside on the pavement."

We suggested that we would not be in his way standing inside.

"I'm sorry," he said truculently. "Nobody's allowed to stand in here until two-fifteen."

And then David let fly:

"Sonny, don't you dare speak to these wounded officers like that! If it wasn't for people like them you wouldn't

41

be parading round dressed like the Admiral of Toytown; you'd be doing forced labour down a German coal mine."

We remained under shelter, but we felt very awkward about the whole thing.

I could not get used to being stared at because of my disablement. Children were the worst offenders, but adults were almost as bad.

Peter Livingstone told me that when he first went about in a half-length plaster cast and his leather collar he was exasperated with these 'gawkers'. Someone else told me that Peter had one day travelled up from the town sitting opposite four small boys who never took their large eyes off him for a moment. Eventually, when he was getting off he turned to them and in a mildly admonishing tone exclaimed:

"You'll get like this too, if you pick your noses."

They told David he was entirely cured and could return to the War Office. He was delighted and invited half a dozen of us to a farewell dinner, with a number of his girl friends to make up the party.

It was a joyful occasion for David and everyone else seemed happy too. It was one of those parties I would have once loved. As I sat there quietly I was thinking bitterly of how I would have laughed and quipped; how I would have interjected bright, witty remarks; how I would have made them rock with laughter.

"Can I cut up your meat for you?" asked the girl sitting beside me.

"Yes, please."

They were planning to go on to a dance. Seven couples; seven men and seven girls.

'I don't need a partner myself,' I thought. 'I need a nursemaid.'

And as dinner wore on I felt more and more like a death's-head at the feast. Why should I go on to the dance? I would only be a passenger. Better to spare myself the humiliation and cut myself adrift from the party. At a convenient moment I slipped out and took a taxi back to the hospital.

I was still awake when David staggered in, very amiable and rather drunk.

"Why did you push off?" he asked. "Weren't you feeling well?"

"I'm all right," I replied.

"You'd have enjoyed the dance."

"What's the good—now?"

He sat on my bed and lit a cigarette.

"Poor old chap," he said quietly. "It must be rather grim. I suppose you're feeling depressed?"

"Yes—and rather a coward."

"You'll have to get used to being like this, Toby. Probably you haven't got the slightest conception how you strike others; if you had, it would give you a lot of satisfaction."

He paused.

"Well?" I asked.

"That girl on your right at dinner. She was sorry you went away. We were speaking about you afterwards. She said how nice you were—how very amusing you must have been before——" he pulled himself up—"at least—not exactly that,"—he tried desperately to put it right. "Don't think she meant——"

"I know perfectly well what she meant," I interrupted. "She meant exactly what she said. That's the hell of it. I'm only twenty-four."

He stood up.

"I was a fool to tell you. I'm sorry. I'm ruddy tactless and I'm drunk as blazes."

He undressed and put out the light without speaking again.

I woke up in the morning feeling in the same mood. After breakfast I received a letter from my late commanding officer informing me I had been decorated 'for gallantry'.

I read it in my room. For a moment I felt a thrill of

pleasure. I wanted to show the letter to David, Dermot, and my closer friends. Then my depression caught up on me again. What was the good? Medals and ribbons were a thing of the past; they meant nothing any longer. It was like being notified you were awarded your rugger colours a year after you had left school. I lobbed the letter into the waste-paper basket. I decided to forget all about it and never to wear the ribbon which I was now entitled to pin on my tunic.

When David had left, the Sister relaxed her rule and allowed Dermot to move into my room in his place. Dermot and I had become very great friends. For my part I admired his easy charm, his perfection of manner; I liked his sense of humour—prematurely cynical, and I found him to be a companion of whom I never tired.

Dermot did not want to go to Lowther Hall Convalescent Home. He had applied for further leave, to spend his recuperation at the little Cornish fishing village where his mother had taken a cottage. It was a bitter blow to him when he was told that he could not possibly make a career of the Army on account of his disability, but arrangements were afoot for him to do a tour, as soon as his recovery permitted, as A.D.C. to the Governor of the Colony where his father was acting as Chief Justice.

Dermot's one brother was serving in Italy, where he had just become engaged to an ambulance driver, a member of the F.A.N.Y.

A week after David had left us our doctor came to our room.

"Well, I've got you two fixed up," he said. "Toby, you're going to Lowther Hall to-morrow, and Dermot's going on leave."

"How long for?" Dermot enquired.

"A month at first. We might prolong it later. You'll have to return for a medical board sometime."

"What about me?" I asked.

"I'm afraid I must be a bit vague with you," the doctor

replied. "First of all you must get absolutely fit for your next operation; then, of course, we'll have to get you on the surgeon's list."

That evening Dermot and I had a celebration dinner as we both felt that we were taking a perceptible step forward on our respective roads to recovery.

CHAPTER VI

FRIDAY was the change-over day between the hospital and the convalescent home.

In the afternoon a small batch of officers and other ranks assembled in the forecourt of the hospital. The party travelled in three or four large ambulances. I happened to be the senior officer present, so I was put in charge of the convoy and I had to travel in the front of the leading vehicle.

All the ambulance drivers were girls—members of the A.T.S. The one sitting next to me was bright and chatty. She asked me where I had been wounded and told me about her own boy friend who was serving in Germany.

"Still, it's nearly over now," she said. "You'll soon get back to your own country."

"Yes," I agreed, not knowing what she was talking about.

"You do speak English well," she went on.

I started to realise the reason for her remarks.

"Do I?"

"Yes. But then I suppose you could speak some before."

"Before what?"

"Well—before you left your own country."

"What country?"

She giggled. "Now you've got me." She glanced at me sideways: "You are naughty asking me that. It might be anywhere—continental, of course. Please don't be offended if I'm wrong. I should say Poland or Czechoslovakia."

Later on a lot of people mistook me for a foreigner. It was quite understandable really, owing to the slow, studied way I spoke and because I paused frequently, unable to pronounce some word.

It took us about three-quarters of an hour to reach

Lowther Hall. Then we swept through the gates and up the long, winding drive.

Lowther Hall was the ancient country seat of a middle-aged baronet. It had been taken over for the duration of the war by the Army authorities as a convalescent home for wounded officers and men of all three Services, who, in fact, were all passed on from the same hospital. About twenty officers lived in the house, and upwards of a hundred other ranks in a hideous hutted encampment in the grounds.

The home has achieved a notable reputation for its eccentric administration, but it served its purpose well and provided ample facilities for getting and keeping fit. The commandant was a brigadier who had, long before the war, retired from the Royal Army Medical Corps; he was as near to being the prototype Colonel Blimp as was possible. The assistant commandant, whose job it was to care for us medically, was a little younger and he had also retired from the R.A.M.C. as a major. I thought at the time that he was the most casual and unsympathetic doctor I had ever come across.

Apart from these two there was a matron, several sisters, a swarm of pretty nurses, the usual quota of physiotherapists and occupational therapists on the medical side, and on the military side a quartermaster and a physical training instructor.

Colonel Blimp received the officers in our party with interest and kindliness; a point with which he seemed particularly concerned was how many of us could play bridge. I subsequently discovered that he was always wondering how he could make the home into a gayer and more sociable place. Apparently it was his constant regret that the only people he ever saw were men who had recently been severely wounded. I heard him proclaiming on this theme once.

"Of course, in the Sudan," he said, "we used to have places like this where officers could come for a holiday.

Great fun they were too—much brighter spirit than you get here. But then," he went on, lowering his voice, "remarkable thing about it, all the chaps who come here seem to have been wounded—most of them badly, too."

Another strange character at Lowther Hall was the butler. His services had been retained by a special arrangement between the baronet and the Army, nominally for the purpose of looking after the owner's property. He was a poker-faced, frock-coated Jeeves who was both hurt and resentful about the intrusion of the Army and the unseemly revolution which had overcome the established order in the Hall. Jeeves had a quaint defensive mechanism which permitted him to completely ignore the fact that Lowther Hall was being run as a convalescent home. He always referred to the patients as 'guests' and he scrupulously over-looked the fact that the Army was in charge.

"Between ourselves, sir," he said to me in my room, "we have a rum lot of gentlemen staying here these days. Sir John used to be far more particular about his guests. I know the country is changing, but it is sad for me to live through it. I used to look forward to my master's house-parties, but now——" he shook his head sadly.

I knew quite a number of people at Lowther Hall. Several had been my contemporaries in hospital and had been in the big ward when I was there. Ralph and George, the two civilians, were both waiting for operations. My difficult Welsh neighbour Captain Rees was still under observation; physically he had recovered, but owing to his mental condition it was inadvisable to send him home. Rees kept absolutely to himself and caused no trouble during the daytime; in the evenings, however, he some-times stood just inside the door of the sitting-room switch-ing the light on and off for as long as twenty minutes at a time; nobody checked him, as we knew he could not help himself, but it was very trying for the people who were endeavouring to read or to write letters.

The boredom and inactivity of life at Lowther Hall made

the place very unpopular. Ralph suggested to me that we put ourselves through a sort of toughening up course, going for increasingly longer walks every day. I willingly agreed, not only because it would pass the time, but also as it would mean we would be ready for our operations all the sooner. Unfortunately poor George was too crippled to join us. I discarded my stick, and Ralph and I were soon walking four and five miles every afternoon.

The officers had no restrictions on their leaving the park. The other ranks were only allowed out three afternoons each week. Most of them regarded the establishment as a kind of prison camp and longed to get away from it; they were always writing to the Press and to their M.P.s about the living conditions. Blimp did not consider their complaints altogether justified.

"Of course accommodation is a bit cramped," he said, "but there are many compensations. Don't know what's good for them, that's the trouble. Lovely country, good food, fresh air—most of them were brought up in the slums anyhow."

Some of us approached him about alleviating the various grievances. But it proved a waste of time.

"It's my show, and I'll run it my own way without your help," he said truculently. "We must have a certain amount of discipline."

Even when the men had their leave, the only place to which they could go was a small country town, twenty minutes' bus ride away.

Blimp, to give him his due, did arrange an occasional E.N.S.A. concert, and a mobile cinema unit visited the home regularly every Friday.

As one might have expected, the atmosphere among the officers was very bad and friction was continuous. We were unfortunate enough to have two rather unpleasant characters amongst us. One was a middle-aged, bearded R.A.S.C. officer who had broken his back when falling off a truck in Belgium. He was extremely fortunate in that he had completely recovered without any after-effects. He considered that it was only his own determination and will-power which had enabled him to get better. Probably, indeed, they were contributing factors, but he seemed quite unable to realise that we did not want to listen endlessly to the history of his courage, and, worse still, he never tired of telling the rest of us that we were retarding our progress by lack of resolution and we might easily recover if we only had the necessary perseverance. Not only was this man a chronic bore; he was also a mischief-maker who went about spreading false and malicious stories.

Another person whom everyone detested was a captain in the R.A.F. Regiment. He was supposed to be suffering from a slipped disc in his spine—later on they discovered there was nothing wrong with him at all and he was returned to duty. He was always fit, strong, and healthy and his favourite pastime was making mock of other people's infirmities. It was a tremendous joke to run off with a pair of crutches and to leave the owner helplessly balanced against a wall. Whenever he heard me talking he used to mimic my struggling speech.

The assistant commandant never checked these unpleasant games and often turned a blind eye to the man's rather heartless practical jokes. It went so far that Peter Livingstone, who had recently joined us and who was the only other R.A.F. officer present, threatened to take up the matter with the man's commanding officer.

When he was leaving he approached me rather self-consciously:

"Peter tells me I have behaved like a complete outsider to everyone."

"You have," I agreed.

"It's the medical people's fault really. I should never have been sent here—it's enough to drive me mad being stuck down here among a lot of broken-down deadbeats. Well, we may meet again."

"I hope not," I said with absolute truthfulness.

50

It took a little time for a newcomer to grow accustomed to the Gilbertian atmosphere of Lowther Hall. During one's early days there appeared to be no limits to the farcicality of the place.

It was one of Blimp's methods of rehabilitation that no matter how badly a man was disabled he should be given no assistance at meal-times; this well suited the butler's make-believe that he was working among a quite normal country household. The consequences were sometimes rather devastating as a number of us had useless or seriously affected arms or hands. It was not at all unusual for a lamb chop to suddenly shoot away, out of control, and slide across the showy-white tablecloth, trailing gravy and cabbage. Immediately the butler would spring forward with poised napkin to repair the damage; Blimp would look aghast, mouth slightly open, his fork arrested and stilled on its journey from his plate; then he would turn to his neighbour, shocked and embarrassed, and talk very much faster than usual. It was really as though one of his officers had eaten peas off his knife with the Viceroy dining in the Mess.

In the beginning I did not speak at meals; I had quite enough to do cutting up my food. This left me ample opportunity for observing my neighbours.

My first dinner I was sitting two places away from Blimp, who always took the head of the table. Whenever the conversation around me flagged I could hear him recounting a story. He was telling how they had allotted him a quarter-master-sergeant to look after the 'Q' side of the Home. Later the authorities had decided the responsibilities warranted a lieutenant-quartermaster on the establishment.

"Would you believe it," Blimp went on. "The sergeant came to me and told me he wanted to apply for a commission so that he could keep on the same job."

I lost some sentences and then:

"Of course, I told him: 'You might get a commission

but that won't make you a gentleman. I won't oppose your application provided you give me an undertaking that you won't expect to ever use the Officers' Mess.' "

I discovered afterwards that the sergeant had given this undertaking. He was now a lieutenant-quartermaster, but used his own little Mess which he shared with the physical training sergeant-major.

Jeeves met me in the hall the following morning before breakfast.

"Sir," he said, "I notice that there is—h'm—something wrong with your arm."

I looked at him in astonishment, as I had heard all about his peculiarities. Indeed, I believe that was the only recorded time he was ever known to depart from his self-deception that it was still peace time.

"I couldn't help noticing at dinner last night. I hope you won't mind me mentioning the matter."

"Of course not," I replied and I wondered vaguely if I ought to make some allusion to a polo accident or a hunting fall just to accord with his fantastic dream-world.

"I was wondering, sir, if we could assist you by cutting up your meals outside."

"It's very nice of you," I told him, "but the brigadier might object."

"The brigadier?" He looked askance.

"Yes, Brigadier ——"

"Oh yes, Brigadier ——"

He pronounced the brigadier's name with the same amount of repugnance as the most abstemious of tee-totallers might feel when pronouncing the word 'whisky'.

"Oh well, in that case, we'll have to leave it."

I soon tired of Lowther Hall and I longed to get on with my operation. Every week a doctor drove out from the hospital to see how we were all getting on. Each time he saw me I pressed him for some decision, but medical men have developed the necessary art of being delightfully non-committal. At the same time I was making my plans to read for the Bar. Someone had typed a letter for me to send to the Director of Legal Studies, the educational supervisor of the Inns of Court. He wrote back that he would like to see me as soon as it could be arranged.

I approached Blimp:

"Would it be possible for me to go to London for the day, sir?"

"I can give passes in special cases," he said. "But are you fit enough?"

"I think so. It's very important business." I waved the director's letter.

"Ah, yes. Your stockbroker, I expect. Well, that's a good enough reason. You'd better have a word with my medical officer; if he agrees, you may go."

I found the assistant commandant playing croquet in the garden. He fell in with my proposal provided I spent two nights in London, one before and one after my day of business. So with the help of my friends, who were very sceptical about the whole thing, I booked a room at a hotel in Kensington and made an appointment with the director.

The war against Nazi Germany ended on the day I travelled to London. I went to bed early, but I was kept awake far into the night by fireworks, shouting and singing. I felt very much out of it all; I imagined myself to be rather like the tangible substance of a nightmare when the sleeper has wakened in the first dim light of the dawn. These people were celebrating, I thought; for them the war with all its hardships was over; they looked forward to a new era and they wanted to forget all that was past. I was just a churlish reminder of what was finished, for the war had left its perpetual imprint on my body. I felt guilty and ashamed amidst all this rejoicing, the way a man feels when he is still wearing a lounge suit and the rest of the company has changed into evening dress.

I spent the following day sitting alone in the hotel. It was the official V.E. Day and I did not feel strong enough to face the milling crowds which were flocking to the West

End; nor, indeed, was I in any mood to join them. I was racked by an uncontrollable bitterness; my position became all too apparent for the first time because I was all alone. No tactful nurses or helpful friends and relatives were there to quietly assist me and to do the innumerable things which I could not do for myself. My helplessness became exaggerated in my mind until I thought of myself as an utterly useless parasite on the community. Worse still, nobody took any notice of me. The people in the hotel seemed to be almost hostile.

I longed for the day to end, and early in the evening I left the excited, crowded lounge for the scant peacefulness of my bedroom. Again the fireworks; again the drunken howls, the singing of war-time songs, the shouting and the dancing. To me it seemed a selfish orgy; they were celebrating from individualistic motives because they had escaped what I had suffered. They were looking at such people as I and saying: 'There but for the grace of God, coupled with my own cleverness, go I. But all that is past and now I must grab, grab, grab whatever I can get out of the future.'

Although the next day was not an official holiday, London was again packed with sightseers when I went down to Lincoln's Inn for my appointment. I was received by a very charming secretary, who showed me into the director's room.

He asked me how and where I had been wounded and seemed incredulous when I told him I had been shot in the head. He had had a son badly wounded during the same campaign; we discussed the conditions in Holland and the evacuation of the wounded. Suddenly the director said:

"So you want to carry on with the Bar?"

"Yes, sir."

"Can you manage it?"

I had intended to lay my cards on the table and I did so. I told him I had been warned that my brain could not possibly stand up to the hard work and examinations, and further, that my voice would never improve sufficiently for public speaking. He seemed remarkably cheerful about the whole thing and recalled how several men with impediments of speech had been quite successful at the Bar.

"Supposing you try the exams," he suggested, "and if you surmount that obstacle, see how much your voice has improved before deciding whether to go into practice or to take some legal appointment."

I thanked him and left his office.

I went back into the Strand. It was hot, stuffy, and thronged with impersonal merry-makers. The bus queues were so enormous that I made my way to Charing Cross. There outside the station I saw the stop I wanted, but here too about fifty people were standing waiting patiently and the few buses which pulled in were already filled to overflowing. I took my place at the end of the line.

I had been standing for about ten minutes when lights suddenly began to dance in front of my eyes, the street rocked and swayed, and the passers-by seemed to be walking along slantwise. I left the queue and staggered off down a side street as there were less people there. I knew I was going to faint, so I sat down in the doorway of a shop.

A couple of Canadian lieutenants walked past. When they saw me they stopped, roaring with laughter; they were both very drunk. One of them came up to my doorway and said:

"Been having one too many, sir? You should know when to stop at your age."

His friend thought this an incredibly amusing remark and they tottered off, howling in merriment.

I waited until I felt a bit better and then went back to the queue, which looked just as long as before. I estimated that I could hold out for five or ten minutes and there seemed to be nothing to do but to wait and hope.

A bus drew in. I heard a girl's voice shouting:

"Two on top and one inside. I'm sorry, that's all."

A murmur of annoyance went up from the crowd. Then the girl's voice again:

"Come on, sir. There's room for you—you, sir, the wounded officer at the end."

People turned round and suddenly I realised they were looking at me. Goodness knows how the conductress had singled me out. Anyhow, I shall always be very grateful to her. I mounted the bus feeling just about done in. There were no seats, but a young girl immediately offered me her place which I thankfully accepted. When I tried to buy a ticket the conductress refused to sell me one. "Not on your life," she said, "we haven't forgotten you yet."

It was a great relief to get back to the quiet, coddled atmosphere of Lowther Hall.

Before dinner that evening Blimp said: "Well, did your stockbroker give you any good tips?"

"I didn't see my stockbroker, sir."

"But you definitely told me—when I gave you leave, 'pon my soul, I'm certain you did. I don't know why you couldn't tell me then what you really wanted." His mounting anger turned to a naughty smile of sympathetic understanding. I imagine he recalled some of the frisky evenings of his own youth.

Very soon after my return I was told that I was ready for my operation. Ralph and George, to their disconsolation, were still kept on the 'toughening up' list.

I returned to the hospital, where I was given a double room on the surgical floor. My companion was a sapper captain from the Guards Armoured Division. I knew him quite well and we had always liked each other. He was called 'Bertie', though that was not his real name and he invariably denied any knowledge of how he had come by it. Bertie had been severely wounded in the head, but not so badly as to require him to leave the Army, which was fortunate as he was a regular officer. We were both to undergo similar operations.

At the hospital life continued much the same as before.

Only the staff had altered; in particular, Boxing Day was no longer there, as her fiancé had arrived home from Burma and they were going to be married straight away.

I picked up *The Times* one morning and saw a notice that Dermot O'Malley's brother had been killed in action in Italy. I knew at once what a tragedy had descended on this delightful, loving, and lovable little family.

The period of waiting seemed more tedious than ever when I was occupying the room from which I would go to the theatre and the bed from which I would see the first light of day when it was all over. It was a great relief when the doctor came into our room and said:

"Well, it's the day after to-morrow, boys. You can toss for who'll be done first. I'm afraid you'll both have to get your hair shaved off again, but never mind, it will all grow again, fine and curly, and the girls love curly hair."

We tossed and I won, so my name appeared first on the operating list.

Bertie, who was inclined in those days to be rather wild, suggested that we should go out for the evening the night before our operations. It was strictly against the rules, as we were supposed to retire early and to swallow a series of pills and go on to a special pre-operation diet.

I went along in the afternoon to be fitted for my plate. The craftsman hammered it into shape on his anvil as I sat alongside.

Then we went out to dinner and had a very drunken evening. We arrived back about midnight to find the hospital in an uproar, and we were immediately summoned in to see the very angry Sister-in-charge. She told us that she would make a full report for disciplinary action to be taken. We were too drunk to care and we both stood there beaming at her with the utmost benignity. All of a sudden she could keep it up no longer and she burst out laughing.

"I shouldn't laugh," she said, "because you have been very naughty; especially you, Toby, as the senior officer of the two. For heaven's sake clear off to bed and we'll forget

57

all about it. And by the way, best of luck to-morrow to you both."

I was so tired that I forgot to take my sleeping tablet. The next thing I knew was that a trolley was being bumped into the room by two orderlies the following morning. Bertie was still blissfully asleep when I was wheeled out. There followed an uncomfortable half-hour while my hair was being shaved off in the ante-room to the theatre, and then the welcome appearance of the anæsthetist with the usual comforting words:

"Just a little prick and you won't feel anything more."

The business of coming round, feeling pain, being sick, was all mitigated by the thought that the operation was over. Now a swift convalescence, and then good-bye to hospitals for ever, I thought.

I enquired the time and a nurse told me it was the middle of the afternoon. Bertie was still in the theatre.

"What was I like, coming round?" I asked the nurse.

"You were sweet," she replied. "You tried to make love to me all the time—you said the most beautiful things."

I never found out if she had spoken the truth; certainly Bertie's conduct when he was regaining consciousness was quite exemplary. He did not come to fully all that day, but was still in a drowsy condition when they gave him a sleeping draught for the night.

We both recovered quickly from our operations and about a month later we were posted back to Lowther Hall. Neither of us had any wish to stay there a day longer than necessary, for we were absolutely fed up with the atmosphere of illness.

After a few weeks we were called back to hospital for medical boards. Bertie was passed fit for home duties in the Army and sent on leave. I had to go through a long session doing tests with a psychiatrist and my board was postponed for twenty-four hours.

The following day I was shown into a room where three R.A.M.C. officers were sitting round a table.

The senior of the three, a colonel, addressed me:

"Well, Tobias, you must be aware that you'll have to be discharged."

"Yes, sir."

"You'll never use your right arm again; you'll always be a bit lame in your right leg, and you'll never be able to speak properly. You've certainly bought it in a big way. Have you any idea what you'll do in the way of work? We suggest farming."

"I'm going to be a barrister."

They all stared at me.

"But that's quite impossible," said the colonel. "What about your voice? And besides, you've been unfortunate enough to suffer a severe brain wound; you'd never pass any exams."

"I'm going to try."

"Well," he shrugged his shoulders, "if you won't take our advice you won't. All I can say is this, don't be too disappointed when you find you can't study—I still think farming's the answer."

Then they told me formally that I was permanently unfit for any form of service whatsoever; that I was no longer required and I would be asked to resign my commission at a later date; meanwhile I was to be sent on indefinite leave pending discharge.

I muttered politely and walked out. Although I had never intended to make the Army my career there was an inexpressible sadness about the finality of the board's decision; the fundamental sorrow which always casts its melancholy shadow over any parting of the ways.

I seemed to realise for the first time what they were taking away from me; my uniform, my commission, and my job. I was to be a civilian, an ex-serviceman; from now on I was no longer a 'brother-officer' to my friends; I was an 'old comrade'; a relationship of the past rather than of the present.

I found Miss Heywood in her room.

"I'm leaving to-morrow," I said.

She stood up. For a moment she shifted her hands nervously and made as if to speak. Then she looked out of the window.

"Well?" she said. "What did they advise you to do?"

"Farming."

"Oh."

"But I'm not going to do it. I'm still going to read for the Bar."

Her face lit up: "Good! I didn't want to influence you in any way. It won't be easy for you—ever. You'll have a hard struggle to study, and even when you have qualified, as you most certainly will, you'll have to keep on fighting against your speech impediment all your life. But I'm sure that when you look back on it at the end, you'll have no regrets. Always remember to have faith in God and that will give you faith in yourself."

I had been trying to think of some words to show how my heart overflowed with gratitude to her for all the wonderful help she had given me. Suddenly I was almost as incoherent as I had been some months previously when I had first met her. However, I think she knew what was in my mind, for she had developed a quite incredible sensitivity through dealing so much with people who were striving to speak, although their shattered voices could no longer communicate any words.

To my surprise and joy I met Dermot O'Malley in the sitting-room. He had also been boarded that day and granted another month's sick leave. It had already been arranged that my mother should rent the small cottage next door to the O'Malleys' in Cornwall, as I was not allowed to travel back to Ireland until I had completed a fairly extensive convalescence by the sea. Mrs. O'Malley was convinced that their little village was the finest place in the world in which to recuperate.

We went into the town that evening, as we had so often done in the past, and we drank to the future in champagne.

I was still supposed to be completely teetotal, but I no longer cared about hospital regulations. In my mind the second lap of the journey had already begun and the past year, with all its bitter memories, was starting to slip back already into the impersonal void which mercifully follows so closely in the footsteps of time.

In the room next to mine a man was delirious. He kept me awake almost the whole night, screaming and shouting. The night nurse knew I would not get much rest and she came in periodically bringing me cups of tea.

After breakfast Dermot and I had a farewell interview with the commandant. Then we said good-bye to all our friends and left the hospital for ever.

CHAPTER VII

PILTON, the beautiful fishing village where Mrs. O'Malley had lived for the past few years, seemed altogether remote from the rest of the world. In appearance it resembled one of those picturesque little ports tucked away cosily in the coastline of Brittany.

Everything about Pilton was warm, easy-going, and friendly. The fishermen, leisurely stacking their tackle or nonchalantly leaning on the rails above the harbour. The artists seated at the water's edge, pleasantly oblivious of all but their inspiration. The well-known playwright who seemed to pass his days idly staring out across the cliffs. Even the residents, strolling about their business and pausing now and then for an amiable chat, seemed to appreciate the joy of living much more than the hurrying, scuttling, bustling townsmen. At times, infected by this lethargy, I used to consider escaping from the future which I had designed for myself and settling permanently in Pilton to try and make a living by writing books. At other times it seemed as though I were not a free agent and I must, of necessity, tread the path which I had been ordained to tread. And then I knew that Pilton was only an interlude, the importance of which in my life was intended only to afford a happy memory on which to look back in times ahead.

We used to leave home every day after breakfast carrying luncheon baskets, books and papers, to walk along the cliffs to a secluded cove, and there we would spend the entire day lying in the sun. I went into the sea and tried to swim; I was delighted to discover that I could use a specially adapted side-stroke which enabled me to cover quite long distances. The pleasure of being able to do one thing at least which normal people could do was indescribable.

Dermot had been offered an instructional job on the staff of the Royal Military College at Sandhurst when he was well enough to start work. Judge O'Malley was at that moment on his way home from Africa to take six months long-overdue leave. Dermot and I used to talk often about his brother who had been killed. He told me his father still refused to believe he was, in fact, dead, as his body had never been recovered, but Dermot himself felt that it was only too true. I sometimes wondered if Dermot's views on his disability differed from mine, as he was a Roman Catholic and I a Protestant. I asked him about it.

"I think," he replied, "that what has taken place all fits into a definite plan. Everyone lives for a purpose, and when that purpose is fulfilled he dies."

I disagreed with him at the time, but later on I decided that there might well be some point in his theory. At any rate the misfortunes which fall on some people might often be designed, not so much for the sake of the victims themselves, but as essential threads of the fabric in the spiritual development of others who come into contact with them.

I had commenced to spend an hour every day copying out a book, to improve my spelling and my left-handed writing. In addition I was dipping lightly into a fairly readable volume on Constitutional Law which the Director of Legal Studies had recommended me to try before I definitely decided whether or not I could stand the strain of concentrated study. I deliberately did not press myself too hard in those early stages.

I had another great surprise. I, like the majority of those I had known in hospital, had made up my mind quite irrevocably that I was marked and damned as a social deformity for the rest of my life. But I soon discovered at Pilton that people largely ignored my disabilities and treated me in much the same way as they treated everybody else. More especially, I had imagined I would appear to girls as a rather frightening ogre, and I was unprepared for their quite unreserved acceptance of my condition. It even seemed that some of them were seeking my company in much the same way as they had done before I became disabled. Gradually it dawned on me that there was no reason why I should feel lonely and apart, and then the barriers with which I had surrounded myself lifted and vanished as cleanly and as joyfully as the mists of the morning being dispersed by the mounting sun.

Judge O'Malley arrived just before Dermot left for Sandhurst. He was one of the sweetest-mannered and nicest men I had ever met. Handsome, slim, and absurdly youthful in looks, he had never lost his soft musical, Dublin brogue. He worried a lot about the son who had been killed—in the judge's opinion he was just 'missing'. Soon after he came to Pilton he sat down with all the correspondence in front of him and set out a well-balanced survey of the known facts to prove to himself that his elder boy was still alive. He asked me to read it through and to comment on it. I wondered what to say. I knew from experience of the infinite care which was taken before a man was officially listed as dead.

I think the judge eventually realised that he was only deluding himself. In spite of his preoccupation, however, he was an excellent and cheerful companion. Whenever he was with us his sense of humour enlivened the whole atmosphere and his modesty and sympathetic approach made it a pleasure to seek his advice.

The judge often teased Dermot gently about his hedonism. He accused him of being cocktail-bar-minded, and when Dermot protested that he liked nothing better than the simple life of Pilton, the judge answered that the way he really wanted to live was with one foot in Pilton and one foot in Mayfair. The judge's other son had intended to be a farmer; the two brothers must have been very different. I used to think Dermot was sometimes swept along by the press and surge of the gay friends whom his magnetic personality invariably attracted around him.

It seemed that the summer would never end and long

after Dermot had gone we were still sunbathing and swimming. I was very, very happy during those months. I had closed my eyes to the future and cut myself off from the past; I was pleasantly suspended in an unrealistic vacuum where time stood still. In the back of my mind I knew that this was but the brief minute when one pauses, gathering one's breath before taking the plunge. Then suddenly one morning the sun seemed dulled and faint; it moved across the sky, not like a chariot, but like the shadow of a chariot; autumn had arrived; the time had come to go forth.

Others too were leaving Pilton, the authors, artists, and conscientious objectors; that little colony of *émigrés* from the battle-scarred cities who had come to continue unstanched the tide of their inspiration—and to escape from the war. I could never summon up the bitter antagonism the majority of the residents of Pilton felt towards them. I thought that they were probably being as true to their own ethical principles as we were being true to ours. I could not help noticing and regretting, whenever I met any of these people, how they were always on the defensive with me and vaguely aggressive—as though they rose involuntarily to meet the onslaught of my resentment, and they backed away suspiciously when they found that the thunder of hoof-beats had been entirely within their own imaginations.

I left Pilton with a premonition that I should return some day many years later when I had fought my individual battle and either lost or won. I still intend to go back, but many things must happen before the propitious moment arrives. I had decided to live in the country just outside London for a few years and to study with private tutors who would understand my peculiar difficulties. The Director of Legal Studies had strongly advised this course, as he deemed it most unsuitable that I should continue my work at a university with all the distractions and diversions involved in the life of an undergraduate.

When I had been discharged from hospital I was told to put myself into the hands of a London specialist who would keep me under observation for a few years. For this purpose I saw Dr. Gatt, a young doctor who had been highly recommended to me. Dr. Gatt seemed to be most impressed with my recovery up to then and was confident that something could be done to improve my arm. He arranged for me to undergo a course of treatment which required my attendance in hospital for three mornings every week for the following six to nine months. I told the doctor of something that had been worrying me a good deal. My experience in hospital had proved to me beyond doubt that recovery was to a great extent dependent on intention and will power. I had always believed, even in the early days after my wound, that I would, sooner or later leave my bed again and walk; likewise I had known that my ability to speak would be restored. But from the start I had doubted whether I would ever be able to use my right arm or hand again. It was useless for people to tell me that I must believe they would recover—one cannot believe unless a state of belief exists in one's mind, and the fact was that I seemed to know that my right arm was doomed. It is possible that this gloomy foreboding did affect my progress; it is also possible a prophetic intuition had insinuated itself into my mind. Anyhow, when I explained all this to the doctor he was reluctant to express his opinion, although he agreed with me that there is a certain point beyond which you cannot control your ideas.

I began my studies immediately and found that my powers to comprehend, to reason, and to remember were largely unaffected, but my tutors told me I was bound to fail any examination unless I could overcome my tendency to leave out words and phrases and to confuse positives with negatives; they pointed out that my handwriting and spelling were deplorable. All these weaknesses were gradually correcting themselves, but the fact remained that I wished to sit for my first exams long before there was any hope of the improvement being substantial enough to make any real difference.

In my spare time I read and went for long walks. I tried as hard as I could to summon up enthusiasm for what had been the pleasures of life before. One evening I was asked to make up a party at a dinner-dance in a West End restaurant. It all seemed surprisingly flat; the reverberations of the orchestra, the tiresome, rather intoxicated people, the conversation of dreary flippancies; the whole thing seemed to be skirting round the fringes of essential, purposeful life. Were these people really enjoying themselves, I wondered, or were they making-believe enjoyment? Why should they hide their souls behind this uniform and brittle mask? I had too long lain in a ward where men's personalities were quite naked and exposed, and clothed no more in the raiment of pretence and deceit. I knew that everybody around that dinner table had a true self which they preferred to keep hidden behind a locked door or concealed by an impenetrable veil. At odd moments, when they were careless enough to leave the door ajar for a second or when a sudden draught momentarily lifted the veil, I almost saw what they really were like. But what I perceived was invariably misery and trouble; they seemed frightened and insecure; somehow they were groping, perpetually groping and never being able to grasp hold of anything tangible. They had no religion and no true philosophy, and consequently they were like falling leaves, drifting aimlessly without purpose or design.

However, I continued to go out whenever I was invited. I had pledged myself to live a normal life, so it was my bounden duty to partake of all the so-called amusements that were conventional to the society in which I found myself. Anyhow, I enjoyed meeting people and, if possible, getting to know them. That was my chief complaint against cocktail-parties, the fact that you did not catch other people's names, neither did they hear yours, and you spent ten minutes in acutely uncomfortable conversation, shout-

67

ing to make yourself understood above the general babble of noise, during which time you were constantly edged and jostled in a mob of compressed humanity. The next morning, when you considered it in retrospect, you remembered the interesting, nameless face of a person who had yelled at you, mostly inaudibly, through a gathering haze of cigarette-smoke. The chances were that you never saw them again, and, even if you did, you were not 'friends', you were simply 'people who had met at a cocktail-party'—an entirely new modern term of relationship denoting the lowest degree of intimacy that could possibly exist. Unfortunately, owing to post-war conditions, especially the shortage of food, cocktail-parties were the only possible method for people to entertain on any considerable scale.

I found a new interest which eventually became all-absorbing. It was music. I began to attend regularly at symphony concerts; at first because I found that they provided an intense spiritual satisfaction and a sense of complete fulfilment which I had not discovered elsewhere; later, I learned to enjoy the technicalities of composition and orchestration. Here was one pursuit in which my disabilities did not hamper my participation in the slightest. When the conductor raised his baton all earthly things slipped aside and I and the rest of the audience were transported into the realms of the composer's fantasy; it was a blissful and harmonious sensation to sit back, completely relaxed, with your mind clear and receptive, and then to fly away, alone but never lonely, free but always guided. At the end of the journey you came back to earth with a sense of peace and beauty; somehow you seemed to have gathered a fulness into your life.

I think that it is one of the fundamental truths of living that the more suffering, the more bitterness, and the more pain which befalls a person, so accordingly is increased their perception and understanding of beautiful things.

Ralph, George, Dermot, and one or two more of us had agreed to meet periodically in London. In fact, George,

Ralph, and I were the only three who used to turn up. I did not blame the others; these reunions were depressing affairs in which all the old, unpleasant memories were fanned into new life. It was strange the way one seemed, at such times, to be treading once again the very early stages of one's ordeal. I found that if I closed my eyes and listened to the two men's voices, I could almost smell the pungent stench of sterilised dressings and the sickly aroma of ether which used to permeate the ward when someone was just back from the operating theatre. I kept on meeting them because I liked their company and I wanted to keep in touch, but the very fact of classing those gatherings as 'reunions' invited a dreary repetition of shop-worn anecdotes and the artificial revival of our common experience.

George had married a nurse from our old hospital. He had settled down at a seaside town teaching at a preparatory school which was owned and managed by his brother. Ralph went up to Cambridge to read law—he was toying with the idea of becoming a barrister too. His career at the university was unhappily cut short as he had a nervous breakdown during his first year and was obliged to leave prematurely. Both George and Ralph were suffering from fairly frequent fits, but very gallantly made light of them when they spoke to me. I think Dermot did not join us because he wanted to forget those dreary months in the surgical ward. I often met him by myself. After a short while at Sandhurst he decided to leave the Army. He told me he found it impossible on account of his lameness to live even a circumscribed Service life.

Dermot loved a gay time and he tried desperately hard to keep pace with the sprightly set with whom he mixed. He told me that on fine afternoons when all his friends went off to the tennis courts and the cricket ground, he used to limp away to his room and lie on his bed with a book—but he did not read; he was all the time listening to the laughter and the distant sounds from the sports fields. So he was going to give it up. I knew what it must have cost him to make that decision. The Army was the career he always longed for throughout his youth; he had been popular and successful in his short Service life and all the avenues to the future would have lain wide open before him if only he had been fit enough to take them. However, a friend of his had arranged a temporary appointment for him at the Embassy in Belgrade; he would be given a chance later of entering the Diplomatic Service properly.

About this time a terrible blow fell on the O'Malleys. The judge was diagnosed as suffering from an advanced, incurable cancer. They had been told that he had only a very short while to live. Judge O'Malley received the news philosophically and said he would prefer to work on right up to the end, so he became president of one of the tribunals to which ex-servicemen may appeal on matters relating to pensions.

Dermot told me about this, standing characteristically by a cocktail bar in a West End hotel. In a few minutes others would be joining us for a light-hearted luncheon-party. I had an inkling then that Dermot was beginning to change; that he was seeking a deeper value in life. It was as though he was starting to look through the bubbles on the top of the champagne and trying to discover the quality and pattern of the glass which was underneath.

All the time people were advising me to change my mind and to take a quiet, secluded job in the country. Only my own family seemed to think that I would be able to pursue the course I had set for myself. At times, when I had my misgivings, it was my family who strengthened me in my purpose. My mother, my brother, and my two sisters all gave me continuous encouragement without which I should have inevitably lost confidence. Furthermore, my brother-in-law, himself a successful barrister, always spurred me on by telling me that there was a place for me in his Chambers whenever I was qualified to go into them.

Just before I was going to take my first exams my tutors raised the matter of my writing again. "It is all very well for us," they said, "but the examiners don't know a thing about you and they will not understand your terrible hand-writing and the way you leave out vital words and constantly mis-spell even the very simplest." Another thing that was worrying me was that the exam papers were very much a race against the clock and writing was for me a slow, laborious business. I decided to send a letter to the examining body stating that I had lost the use of an arm and enquiring whether I could possibly be allowed a little extra time on the papers. I received a prompt and courteous reply telling me that my request could not reasonably be granted, but offering me the use of an amanuensis, someone who would write down my answers in a private room. I declined the suggestion as I imagined it would be too difficult to dictate my thoughts in any reasoned, compact form. My tutors were angry with me and told me that the amanuensis provided my only hope of getting through. They persuaded me to write again, saying that I would like to avail myself of his services.

I woke up on the examination morning feeling unbelievably calm. It was a lovely spring day and the country looked fresh and beautiful. All the way up to London in the train I wondered why I was not worried by thoughts of the papers which I was to sit. My feeling was not at all one of over-confidence; on the contrary, the exams had suddenly become of little importance and it did not seem to matter whether I passed or not. And yet some power, some infinite strength, seemed to have taken charge of my body and mind for the day and to be easing away the obstacles which lay in my path.

When I arrived at the examination hall I was shown into a small room where Mr. Polden, the amanuensis, was sitting. We had a preliminary discussion in which he was very kind and helpful. He told me he had been doing this sort of thing for over twenty years and had started by helping disabled students after the First World War. His clients whom he admired most of all, he said, were the

71

blind, who learnt by braille. Suddenly he pulled out his watch and waited until the hand was on the hour.

"Right," he said, "we'll begin now."

He took out a sealed envelope, tore it open and extracted the first paper. I read it over, marking the questions I would answer. Then we started. He took down at my dictation in large copper-plate handwriting, the characters of which he formed with incredible ease and speed. At the end of each page he handed me the sheet of foolscap to check over and to suggest any alterations. Only once did he pause for a short rest; and then he produced a thermos flask of coffee and two mugs. I took my mug across to the window. Outside was a quiet Lincoln's Inn Square with people strolling nonchalantly past. I looked back at Mr. Polden.

"I'm ready to go on when you are," he said.

Really, I thought, this was not like an examination at all.

At the end of the allotted time he folded up the pages of writing and sealed them in an envelope. I made my way to my Inn of Court. It was rather disturbing in the students' lunch-room because everyone was running over the morning's paper and mentioning points which I had left out in my answers. At two o'clock, Mr. Polden and I met again in the small room and then went through the same procedure all the afternoon.

That evening I went through my answers with my brother-in-law, who told me I should have provided enough material to ensure a pass. At any rate, I would not know any more until the results were published some five weeks later. I was leaving for Ireland the following week to take a short holiday and to continue my studies over there until the end of the summer. For me Ireland was the past, and England the present and the future, and I wanted to explore again the once-familiar haunts of my early years. Indirectly, I suppose, it was partly the customary whim of the sentimentalist, but in part it was because I felt that over there I would gain a new strength by assuring myself I was the same person who had once enjoyed the greatly maligned blessing of being inconspicuously ordinary.

People often used to ask me what was the greatest inconvenience of being one-armed. Invariably they suggested writing and knotting a tie. In fact, the doing of both these things causes very little inconvenience at all and in reality the greatest nuisance—it is nothing more than a nuisance—is being continuously like a normal person holding a bulky parcel in one hand. It follows that when the one-armed man carries anything in his good hand, a book, a coat, or an umbrella, he becomes like an ordinary person carrying objects in both hands. It is a comparatively rare thing for anyone who is able-bodied to travel across a town, using Tube trains and buses, without keeping at least one hand free, and they do not at first comprehend the extreme difficulty of balancing yourself whilst walking down the gangway of a moving bus or extricating yourself from the crowd clustered round the entrance of an Underground train. Another thing which I found very awkward was sorting out a bundle of loose change, an essentially two-handed job. Sometimes in a bus I delved into my pocket and took out a collection of coins; the problem from there was how to select those that I needed. My disability was by no means obvious and occasionally, when I suggested to the conductor that he might pick out the necessary money, he became irritated and replied: "Feeling tired, chum?" or some similar ironical comment. Of course, many conductors were understanding and helpful and quickly realised why I had made this unusual request.

I think the one-armed man plans ahead in little things to an extent which few people would realise. How shall I carry my suitcase and paper, and be able to show my ticket? What shall I do with my umbrella when I am opening the carriage door? The world was designed for the normal person, and there are surprisingly few gadgets to help one who is physically abnormal. I sometimes wonder whether it would not be worth while for some firm to visualise day-to-day life for the one-armed and to devise every sort of implement which would help them and would alleviate many of their problems. There must be very large numbers who would eagerly avail themselves of such assistance.

I have always found that the average individual is fundamentally kind and sympathetic. Very often he suffers from self-consciousness and embarrassment when confronted by the disabled. It would help enormously if everyone realised that the greatest wish of a disabled person is to be treated, as far as possible, as though he were physically normal. It is a mistake to fuss; it is a mistake to make a conscious, noticeable effort to help. In the early days I only became ill-at-ease when people were bustling round me; I used to think: 'What a nuisance I am, upsetting everyone so much.' On the other hand, there were certain people who appeared at the time to be oblivious of the fact that there was anything wrong with me at all; on looking back afterwards I used to realise how careful they had been to make everything easy; how gracefully and naturally I had been offered a comfortable chair; was it mere chance that there was a small table on the correct side, ready to hold my tea-cup? And when the others suggested making up a tennis four, there was no embarrassing moment in which they begged me to join in, because my hostess had forestalled them by offering to show me round the garden while they played.

By now I have become used to holding something in my good hand, for instance a cocktail glass, when I am being introduced to a person. Sometimes they thrust out their hand for me to grasp. I have to shake my head and mumble something about not being able to use my right arm. Very often they immediately become terribly confused and behave as if they had been guilty of an extremity of tactlessness. If only they knew how quickly you come to accept your disability and lose all your initial self-consciousness about it. Your deformed limb becomes part of you, and, as you live with it day after day, night after night, you gradually forget that it has ever functioned properly at any time. If there were some people born with three arms, I suppose all the others with only two would consider that they laboured under something of a handicap; I do not think their feelings on the matter would be any stronger than that.

CHAPTER VIII

IRELAND has always been a legendary, fairy-tale country. Just after the war it was possessed of the fantastic, magical quality of a dream. Eire had thrived on her neutrality and achieved a state of prosperity I had never seen in her before. I did not blame anyone for this, for I have always fervently believed that it is a basic right in any civilised conception of any just international system that every small nation must have unfettered liberty to elect neutrality in a general conflict. Although hundreds of thousands of men and women had crossed the border or the channel from Eire to join up, there was not the general after-the-war atmosphere which you found in England. People seemed to be happier and more confident; in a way it resembled the blissful confidence of immaturity—that artificial sense of security which is worn like a comfortable cloak until the harsh fingers of experience suddenly rip it from your back. Still, it was novel and refreshing to talk to people who had not cowered in air-raid shelters or weathered the storms of the fighting line.

In due course I heard that I had passed my first batch of exams, so I made plans to sit for the next lot after the summer. Although I was working quite hard I had plenty of time to enjoy the simple pleasures of the seaside village where I was staying. I knew quite a number of people living all around—warm-hearted, hospitable, friendly folk, and the weeks were filled with picnics, tennis-parties and an occasional private dance. The local residents were great yachtsmen; for a long time the Yacht Club had formed the centre of social activity. Now, however, political feeling had usurped purely sporting instincts and the club was in the hands of a group of intensely nationalistic young men. As a result, when my uncle tried to get me elected for the

76

season as a temporary member, he was unsuccessful. For one thing, I was an ex-officer of the hated British Army, and for another, my family was supposed to have Unionist traditions, although as far as I was aware my father, who had spent almost his whole life in India and South America, had taken as completely a detached attitude to Irish politics as my brother and I had done ourselves. It was difficult at times to comprehend how parochially the Irish approached their affairs; they seemed to imagine that their personal problems dominated the thoughts and conversations of the whole world as much as they dominated their own. I suppose it is easy, when you are used to living in a country whose independence has flourished proudly for generations, to criticise a new republic, revelling in the first flush of nationalism. But I was saddened by the extremities to which patriotic feeling was pressed: the foredoomed attempt to revive the Gaelic language; the spirited endeavour to exclude all foreign influence from sport, art, and culture; and the deliberate effort to circumscribe the national outlook to the limits of the country's borders. I regretted all this because I longed to see a universal policy of internationalism spreading throughout the war-scarred world, although, at the same time, I in no way begrudged this small nation her independence, which she had won at the end of a long and valiant struggle.

Of course I always refused to become mixed up in any political discussions, and I can only recall one instance when I departed from this practice. My London doctor wanted me to continue treatment for my arm for a bit longer, even though it had so far failed to produce any beneficial results. I had arranged to attend a hospital in a near-by town two or three times every week. I always saw the same physiotherapist, an extremely cheerful and efficient girl. When she went away for her summer holiday, my treatment was taken over by another girl, a member of one of the most fanatically nationalistic families in the town. She had grown up in the shadow of political hatred

because her father had been one of the patriot leaders during
the final struggle against England, and had been killed in a
raid on his own home. Even at that moment her brother
was serving a long sentence on account of some shooting
affray with the Eire police; he belonged to an extreme
group which was displeased with what they considered the
over-moderate policies of their present government. She
was an attractive little thing and I took an immediate liking
to her.

One afternoon when I was having my treatment this girl
suddenly looked up and said:

"Do you call yourself English or Irish?"

"Irish," I replied.

"I thought so," she said. I could see her anger mounting
and the colour rising in her cheeks. She told me I had no
right to regard myself as an Irishman, for I had forfeited
every claim I ever possessed when I had fought for England
in the recent war. In vain I pointed out that I had never
fought for England against Germany; in fact I had fought
for democracy against totalitarianism; that principles
affected me far more than nationalities—but she would
have none of it. We argued for an hour, and eventually
when I left her the waiting-room was full of very impatient
people, waiting for long-overdue appointments.

A week later I met her in the main street of the town and
she dashed up and apologised.

"I was very foolish," she said. "It's a gross breach of
professional etiquette to discuss politics or religion with a
patient."

I told her that I had not minded at all, and we went off
and had tea together. I could not help thinking how tragic
it was for this charming young girl to be mentally distorted
by such a deep and terrible bitterness.

While I was in Ireland the British Ministry of Pensions
arranged a medical board for me over there. It was a casual
affair and, as far as I could see, I was the only patient who
was attending on that occasion. A middle-aged doctor

examined me and asked me a lot of questions, the answers to which he wrote down on a form. His manner from the start was easy and amiable, but it altered at one point and he became almost paternal as he lowered his voice.

"Let's have a heart-to-heart chat," he began, with a forced, beaming smile, intended to put me entirely at my ease. "You know, old chap, you can trust me implicitly—I mean one mightn't talk about this with most people, but with me—I think we can rely on one another not to break a confidence."

"Well?" I asked unhelpfully, expecting to be cross-examined about all the youthful indiscretions I had ever committed.

He leant towards me and whispered dramatically:

"Do you ever hear voices?"

"Voices?" I echoed blankly.

"Yes, voices—when nobody is there."

"Like Joan of Arc?" I suggested.

He was taken aback for a moment, then he seized eagerly on my answer.

"That's right; so you do?"

"No," I said emphatically.

He tried again:

"Tell me about any peculiar experiences you have had."

"What sort of thing?"

"Well, like footsteps following you in a dark street at night."

I did not know whether to be amused or angry.

"Are you trying to make out I'm round the bend?" I asked him.

He was most conciliatory.

"Oh dear no, I was only fishing. You know, after so severe a head wound as yours one has to make certain."

Later he asked me why I was so insistent on becoming a barrister and I told him, quite truthfully, that one of the reasons was so that people in future would not wonder, as he had done, if my injury had left me a bit simple. I discovered afterwards that he was the medical superintendent of the local lunatic asylum.

Ministry of Pensions medical boards in England were more formal. Pensioners are treated at them with a degree of courtesy and helpfulness which would provide a very useful example for many other government departments. From the doctors down to the clerks and the liftmen, everybody seems to be doing their utmost to assist. I do not know who was responsible for the happy inspiration of choosing the commissionaire who has stood, ever since the war, outside the Ministry's London office in Euston Square; I do know, however, this man's sympathy, good-nature, and helpfulness must have warmed the hearts of thousands of pensioners going for their periodical boards.

Summer passed quickly and it was soon time to return to England. My mother had taken a London flat; although I knew I would stand a better chance of keeping fit in the country, I decided to go and live with her because I felt that I should begin to get used to living in a city as soon as possible, as almost my entire working life would most likely be spent in one. I went to London in October intending to sit for my next exams in December. As far as I could see, the new surroundings did not cause me any inconvenience at first.

After a few weeks in London, I definitely decided that I was going to suffer from none of the rather unpleasant complications which I had been warned were possible for five years after a head wound. Then, in a moment, all the gloomiest forebodings were revived in their fullest magnitude. It happened when I was walking down Oxford Street one afternoon. I had been feeling odd, indescribable symptoms of uneasiness for the past hour, and now quite suddenly I felt I was going to pass out. My head went hot and cold and there was a reeling sensation and lights. I saw a taxi pulling up beside me so I jumped in quickly and asked the driver to take me home. A short while later I had recovered, but the whole thing had been extremely unsettling and, what is more, in an indefinite sort of way, I was not feeling at all well. I decided to try to forget about the experience; probably after a night's rest, I thought, the vivid reality of it would recede into the trivial half-remembered background.

But the next day I had not forgotten, and I could not escape from an uncomfortable presentiment that I was in for a lot more trouble. When I went out after breakfast I almost fainted again and I had to return home to lie down. My doctor came round to see me and recommended that I visit one of the neuro-surgical specialists whom I had known in the hospital. This was promptly arranged and an appointment made for the following week.

In the meantime I began to feel more and more ill; it was almost impossible to do any work under these conditions and I had my exams within the following three weeks.

The neuro-surgeon put me through a very thorough examination. Then he made me sit down.

"There is nothing new," he said, "and, unfortunately, nothing much we can do about it. This probably would have happened in any event, but it is quite likely it has been worsened by the mental strain of studying. I recommend that you give up your work—at any rate for a couple of years. You cannot possibly take your next examinations."

I begged him to let me take them and then go off for a long holiday until the spring, when I could resume quietly. However, he was adamant.

"We are feeling our way with the post-operative care of people who have had operations like yours," he said. "Frankly, we don't know much about your future prospects. It has been impossible to gain any experience, because you are the first batch of patients to have undergone such far-reaching surgery and lived through it. We have given you your life, why not be thankful and leave it at that? That's all I can say—be content with the miracle that you are still alive and give up any ambitions for the future."

81

It was a terribly difficult decision to make. From one point of view I had tried and failed; I could now abandon the attempt with good grace; from another, this trouble, quite possibly, had not been brought on by studying and my illness might disappear as suddenly as it had come on. Eventually I decided that I would take the exams and settle the future later on when I was feeling better.

I was unable to get around on my own because these fainting attacks were becoming more and more frequent, so I arranged with a private hire car to take me to the examination hall in the morning, and to collect me again in the evening. Mr. Polden and I spent a day in the same room as before and at the end, feeling completely exhausted, and knowing I had failed the papers abysmally, I went home.

I had thought that when the exam was over I would immediately feel better; in fact I became worse and worse. Insomnia and severe headaches were added to my other troubles, until it seemed sometimes that I would never again be fit to do even the very easiest and lightest of jobs.

I went for a holiday to the seaside with one of my sisters. The mental anguish was dreadful. I had reached a stage when I dare not go out by myself and I did not care much to be alone even indoors. It was invidious and humiliating to be like this. There is not much honour about going around with a smashed-up body as a result of war wounds, but there is not even a pretence of glory about a smashed-up mind—it becomes a subject for whispered comment; for pity mingled with revulsion.

The exam results were published—I had passed. This only made my problems even more difficult. If I had failed, if my greatest efforts had borne no fruit, the choice might have seemed obvious, for I had blissfully imagined that I could master and overcome the concerted after-effects of my wounds, and when it had been effectively proved that I was wrong there would have been no alternative but to resign myself to the inevitable. Now, however, I saw clearly that this attack had not affected the standard of my work.

If I was to suffer this mental condition indefinitely, even then there was no reason why I should be unable to do a normal job. But I had hopes that this was only a phase through which I must pass before my recovery was complete; already I imagined the unpleasantness was easing slightly in intensity.

I returned to London and saw Dr. Gatt again. I told him I had decided to carry on; that my whole purpose of life was bound up in the fulfilment of my present plan.

"And what of the future?" he asked.

"I will not look ahead any further," I replied. "When I'm qualified I'll think out the next step."

I explained how I thought I was getting better. I asked him if it was possible that my liability to fainting fits would vanish.

"There is just a chance," he said. "The trouble may be caused by a healing scar on the surface of the brain. In that case it should be completely all right in a matter of months."

He agreed that I should return to Ireland—not to work but to relax completely. He left it to my discretion whether to start studying again if I felt well enough.

I went to stay in a very quiet, isolated part of the west coast of Eire. I spent my whole time out-of-doors, walking, swimming, sun-bathing, and taking out a small boat with one or two friends. There was nothing spectacular about my recovery, but very slowly and very gradually I stopped getting such frequent headaches; I passed entire days, and then entire weeks, without any fainting attacks, and I started to sleep without any trouble at nights. At the end of four months I felt ready to carry on.

I had resolutely shut my eyes to what I would do when I had finally qualified. It seemed to be better to feel my way with very limited objectives rather than to plan on a long-term overall policy. Of course, in the back of my mind, I always knew that nothing would satisfy me except a full and normal life as a practising barrister.

I stayed on in Ireland for another few months until I was definitely satisfied that the trouble was over; then I returned to London.

There was only one further exam before I began to work for my finals. I took this in the winter with the assistance, once again, of Mr. Polden, and once again I was successful. There lay ahead a long period of protracted study which left little time for anything else as most of my evenings were taken up in reading text-books. However, I was happy enough to be able to live like an ordinary person once more, and the time passed very quickly.

I wanted to sit my last examinations without an amanuensis; all my earlier difficulties with my spelling and omission of words had disappeared and I could now write fairly legibly at a reasonable speed.

One Saturday morning, a short time before my finals, Ralph rang me up:

"George and I are going to a theatre this evening and having dinner together afterwards. Why don't you come along too?"

I told him I had intended to work that evening, but eventually he persuaded me to join them. I was in the throes of my final revision, with the exams commencing in just over a month's time. At any rate there did not seem to be any harm in taking a few hours off, especially as I had been driving myself pretty hard for some months past.

I met George and Ralph at the latter's club; we had a drink and then went to the theatre. Half-way through the performance I began to feel peculiar. I wondered if I had been over-working. Throughout the second half I felt worse and worse, and I came to the conclusion I was very definitely running a fairly high temperature. I did not want to spoil the evening for the others, so I said nothing about it. I was hoping that a couple of stiff drinks before dinner would pull me round, and certainly they did grant me a slight temporary easement. At last I could stick it out no longer, so I made my apologies and took a taxi home. I longed to get into bed and rest my head on the pillows, but when I did so I found they provided small comfort, because even when I closed my eyes I could not escape from the swirling, tumbling motion, as though I was in a plane flying through never-ending air pockets. Eventually I went off to sleep, a troubled sleep riddled with nightmares and broken by continual waking to an atmosphere of sweaty discomfort.

The following morning I felt really ill, so I remained in bed. I refused to call in a doctor; it seemed so vital that I should recover quickly and be able to carry on working the next day, and I was afraid my doctor might order me to take a week's rest; that, at that moment, appeared to be as great a catastrophe as could be imagined. I dressed for tea, but afterwards I had to return to bed because I was feeling so bad. Quite by chance a cousin of mine, who was a surgeon at a London hospital, came in to see me in the evening and insisted on taking my temperature.

"Just as I thought," he said, looking at the thermometer, "there's something very much the matter here. You must call in your doctor immediately."

When my doctor came and examined me he told me I had pneumonia and I would be in bed for at least a fortnight, during which time I must not open a book.

"Can I still take my finals next month?" I asked.

"I would prefer to say nothing definite about that for the time being," he replied. "It will depend to a great extent on how quickly you can get over this—and, of course, the absence of complications."

I passed through the crisis of the illness satisfactorily and I was well on the way to recovery when I contracted pleurisy.

"That settles it," my doctor told me. "You will not be fit even to travel to the examination-room by the date you have mentioned."

I begged him to write to the examining body saying that, although I would have recovered sufficiently to sit the exam, the only factor which prevented me from doing so was my inability to travel. Eventually he agreed to do what I asked, but he assured me he did so with some reluctance as, in fact, he had considerable doubts whether I would be well enough to stand the strain of examination conditions.

The Secretary of the Council of Legal Education wrote in reply that, provided I was sufficiently improved, it would be possible for me to take the exam at home with Mr. Polden acting as combined invigilator and amanuensis.

The final examination for the Bar lasted for three intensive days, with a three-hour paper each morning and another every afternoon. Mr. Polden settled himself at the desk in my bedroom. I had dressed for the first time since my illness and I sat in an arm-chair. At the appropriate time he unsealed the first paper and handed it to me, and for the next few hours I dictated to him. After lunch I was feeling the strain and it required a considerable effort to finish the afternoon's work. When it was over I went straight to bed. On the next two mornings Mr. Polden returned again and I struggled through the morning and afternoon papers feeling cumulatively weary. Looking back when it was all finished, I realised how the questions in every paper appeared to be almost designed to cover the parts of the work I knew best. All the same, I felt very depressed about the result, because I had been almost too tired to think after the first couple of hours each day.

Dr. Gatt advised me, if it turned out that I had failed, not to sit the exam again.

"There are limits beyond which you cannot push yourself," he said, "and frankly, you have almost reached breaking point."

He wanted me to go away immediately for a long holiday in Ireland, but I insisted on waiting until the results were published so that I could make my arrangements accordingly.

Roderick Shackleton, my brother-in-law, offered to send one of his pupils to look at the examination lists when they were posted in the Council of Legal Education Chambers, the day before they appeared in the newspapers. In the afternoon the telephone-bell rang. I lifted the receiver:

"Is that Mr. Tobias?"

"Speaking."

"Mr. Shackleton would like a word with you."

Then Roderick's slow drawl:

"Hullo, Toby, you've got through."

"Thanks," I said lamely, feeling completely at a loss for words.

I replaced the receiver. My first reaction was a wild rush of excitement. This was the moment to which all my hopes, my struggles, and my aspirations had been directed ever since my recovery from my wound. Then my ecstasy died away. It was not myself, I realised, who had done this thing; it was another far mightier force working through me. I ought not to feel any pride; my mood ought merely to be one of thankfulness. In that moment I saw clearly how little can be achieved by mortals; they are solely the medium by which the Divine Will is exercised. But I rejoiced that if God had brought me so far, He might lend me His help to fulfil whatever was destined for me on the remainder of my journey through life.

Roderick invited me to dine with him at his club the following evening.

"The time has come to think out the next move," he said.

During dinner he told me the various possibilities. He advised me to go with him as his pupil for a year. After that, he said, I would be invited to join his Chambers, and to practise from them. Those particular Chambers had a plentiful supply of work and a place in them was greatly to be coveted by any young barrister. As an alternative, I might forsake the wear and tear of practice at the Bar and, if I preferred, he would help me to find a job as a legal adviser in industry, or as a legal assistant in some government department. I made my choice without difficulty—

I wanted to practise. I asked him if he thought my voice would be an insuperable handicap.

"Personally, I don't think so," he replied. "It has improved enormously during the last year or two. You'll have to brace yourself for a tremendous ordeal before you get used to talking in Court. It is hard enough for people who've never had any sort of trouble with their speech—you, of course, will have all the added worry of knowing you have to overcome an impediment."

My own opinion was that, with any defect of speech, the more you push yourself the more you gather confidence, and so accordingly your disability diminishes. I thought of Winston Churchill and King George VI, who had both refused to succumb, and had at length overcome their vocal handicaps.

We settled my future there and then over the dinner table. I would have to go away first and build up my strength as my illness had left me in a very low condition. My Inn of Court had granted me permission to be called to the Bar by proxy, so that I would not have to wait in London for that event to take place. I would, however, have to get my Call papers signed by a Bencher of my Inn. Roderick arranged for me to go and see Mr. Justice Tremayne, a High Court judge, who was a great friend of his.

I visited the judge in his room in the Law Courts. I had often heard he was one of the kindest and most charming people anyone could wish to meet, and my interview certainly bore this out. He went out of his way to put me at my ease, and so did the other judge who shared his room with him. They were, at that time, two of the youngest and most popular High Court judges who sat on the Bench. I always cherish that occasion and I will never forget it, because I felt then an inner glow of pride that I was now a member of a profession where men at the very top could take so much trouble over one at the very bottom. When I was leaving, they both told me that at any time in the future, if I was in need of any help or any advice, I was to come back to that room and they would be only too willing to do everything possible to assist me. It would have been easy to dismiss those words as the empty and meaningless phrases of a practised tongue, but as it happened my life did not entirely separate from either of these judges, and the occasion was to arise when each of them would prove that he had really meant what he had promised.

At various times in your life your path crosses that of someone whose personality and character tower above those of his fellows. He seems to move with a brighter light; to live on a broader plane; to fulfil himself to a deeper purpose. You know at once that you are meeting one of those rare people who have achieved a permanence and durability completely in defiance of the all-obliterating law of the universe.

As I left the Law Courts I was thinking, in all humility, that when our legal system could produce judges as matchless as the two I had just met, we had every reason to proudly believe that our Bench was the finest in the world.

Having made all my plans for the following year, I crossed to Ulster, where I had arranged to stay with some relatives in Belfast for the week of the Royal Ulster Show. My cousin was a member of the committee running the Show and consequently, each day we attended, we did so in great comfort. It was a complete change, after being immersed in law so absolutely, to hear the discussions on horses and cattle, and to watch the skilful grace of the international jumping contests.

From Belfast I went on to County Donegal to spend a couple of months at a hotel by the shores of Lough Swilly. I was so determined to recover my fitness in the shortest possible time that I spent my days swimming, walking and climbing small mountains. In the back of my mind I was puzzled by the persistence of the weak feeling, which I was never able to shake off completely after my attack of pneumonia. Also, no matter how hard I might try, I could not persuade myself that I was really either enjoying my holiday or feeling in any way better as a result of my active, open-air life. And yet this sort of living had always put me right before; there seemed to be no reason why it should not do so again.

I was then twenty-eight years old. Once, many years previously, I had enquired of somebody, many years my senior, at what stage in a man's life he ceased to be entitled to the epithet of 'young'. He had replied:

"You remain a young man until the day another man younger than yourself addresses you as 'Sir'."

I recalled this conversation one evening in the bar of the hotel. A youthful undergraduate from Queen's University, Belfast, came up to me with the fatal words:

"Can I buy you a drink, sir?"

A short while later I went outside to watch the sun setting over the Lough. Long inroads of black shadow mingled with the golden patches on the water, and the distant mountain glimmered and sparkled in a last quicksilver glow, before the sombre nightclouds would hide it from view.

In the early Latin primer I had used at my preparatory school had occurred a phrase, illustrating some grammatical construction. It had run:

"Age will come with quick step and silent tread."

I had been so busy during the last few years that I had not noticed my youth gradually slipping away from me. I did not grieve a great deal at its passing, but there was an inherent sadness about this moment. I suppose it comes like that to everyone. A casually dropped word; a glance in the mirror; the look in the eyes of a stranger. And then a moment of realisation.

The irony of youth is that you do not appreciate its quality until it has left you; it is only then you perceive the infinite beauty and fascination of the lithe, easy movements of youthful bodies; the fleeting, shimmering lights that dance across youthful faces; and the eager, fresh ideas which pirouette through youthful minds. It is the eternal law that the old must revere the young; and an eternal sorrow that the young will one day—all too soon—become old themselves.

Perhaps some of the years which should have been the brightest and best of my life had been weighed down prematurely by delicacy and illness. I could now face up to a thought such as that without any bitterness or any regret. For I was beginning to understand how deceptive material values could be. Surely there was a far more real happiness to be gained from spiritual than from physical pleasures? I was certain that what appeared to be a great and terrible disaster might easily become a tremendous re-awakening. In the scheme of things the balance is heavily tilted on the side of misfortune; one may only achieve an infinite and lasting contentment by adjusting oneself to meet the powers of sorrow on their own chosen battlefield.

I soon realised that, as my holiday wore on, I was not recapturing my health; on the contrary, I was steadily becoming worse. I made an appointment with Dr. Gatt and hurried back to London. He told me that it was apparent that something had gone wrong.

"It is not your head wound this time, it is your chest. Your brain injury, thank goodness, is not likely to cause any more trouble. After you were wounded, your chest seemed to have healed up so perfectly that nobody thought it was necessary to do anything about it. It seems they were wrong. But I still do not think it will be anything very serious."

He arranged for me to be X-rayed the following day and added that, if it was necessary, he would hand my case to a leading chest specialist.

I was not very worried about the matter because I felt that Dr. Gatt would put things right as quickly and as surely as he had always done in the past. Meanwhile I could complete my arrangements for starting in Roderick's Chambers.

The following week Dr. Gatt rang me up.

"Well," he said, "I've seen your X-rays. Unfortunately there is something very serious. I'm fixing up for you to see Dr. Roberts."

I pressed him for more details. At first he seemed reluctant, then, seeing that I refused to be put off, he said:

"The chest is a very delicate organism. You were unlucky when you got wounded. The damage never really mended, and it has now turned into a tuberculous infection."

"You mean I've got T.B.?" I said, aghast.

"You'll get over it," he replied. "It's nothing to what you've been through already."

It struck me later that, as I had been as close to death as one can possibly be, this last remark provided little comfort. I felt completely stunned. The trouble with tuberculosis is that the general public knows so little about it. I at once imagined that Dr. Gatt was telling me my death sentence, and I thought vaguely that T.B. specialists graded all their patients in terms of 'so many months to live'.

My friends and my family would not believe that the diagnosis was correct. They half persuaded me by way of numerous examples about people they knew who had had similar alarms which had eventually proved to be quite unfounded.

Dr. Gatt had told me to keep very quiet, and I was feeling so ill that I had no wish to disobey his instructions.

I went up to Harley Street one evening for my appointment with Dr. Roberts. He was a middle-aged Welshman who, at first, struck me as being slightly distant and over-pompous; I was later to alter my view completely, when I discovered that he was the epitome of kindliness and possessed a never-failing sense of humour. At any rate, from the first he inspired me with a tremendous confidence in his capabilities. After a meticulous examination, he told me to sit down, and he seated himself at a desk, scribbling notes. He seemed awkward and a little embarrassed; the atmosphere of his consulting-room was charged with his seriousness.

"I'm afraid I've got some very unpleasant news to break to you," he began.

"Have I got T.B.?" I cut in.

"Unfortunately your wound has caused tuberculous trouble."

I could see that, in spite of the fact that he must have broken this news to thousands of people over the course of a score of years, he was still grimly conscious of the awful effect the name of this disease could produce.

"Is it very bad?" I asked.

"Frankly, I cannot tell until I know how well you will respond to treatment. But we must fight this thing together, you and I—I will do all that medical science will enable me to do—the rest is up to you."

He then told me I would have to go into the Broadway Hospital in North-East London as soon as he could procure a bed for me, and after that, in due course, he would like me to go down to the Hedgely Sanatorium in Sussex.

"I will do whatever you wish," I assured him, "but can you possibly tell me how long my treatment will last?"

He got up, crossed over, and put his hand on my shoulder.

"No," he said quietly. "No. We mustn't think of time. Your career and your future must be put out of your mind. I want all your concentration and all your strength for the tremendous fight you and I are going to make."

He showed me out to the front door. It was then about six o'clock in the evening. He advised me to take a taxi home, but there were none about, so I walked up to the top of Harley Street and caught a bus. I was to go straight to bed when I arrived home, and I was to stay there indefinitely—months or years.

"Rest is our chief weapon," he had said. "Bed and complete and absolute rest."

My bus route lay through the West End. The shops, the lights, and the people. I watched it all avidly. I had suddenly realised how wonderful life could be—just life, normality, brightness and movement.

An hour later I was in bed. I felt tired and ill, and even with this dreaded disease it was a relief to know that I was at last under treatment. The gnawing doubt in my mind was stilled; the impossible struggle to make-believe I was well was ended; all my troublesome symptoms were now crystallised into this one definite fact—I had tuberculosis.

I lay awake for most of that night, and by the following morning my mind had adjusted itself to my new predicament. I had fought for my life before this, and I was ready to renew the battle. Faith and prayer had won me through last time, and I would fall back on those two terrific sources of infinite strength once again. It was no good worrying about the Bar; that would all come later—I had first of all to conquer this new enemy.

My family and friends were once again magnificent. They visited me, amused me, cheered me up. I was inspired by their courage, and gradually I became filled with a new confidence and hope.

Three weeks later I received notification from the Broadway Hospital that there would be a vacancy for me in a double room on the following day. There were very few preparations to be made because they advised me not to bring any outdoor clothes as I would not be up at all. I went round to the hospital in a taxi with one of my sisters. It was pleasant to be dressed again, even if it was for such a brief time.

The Broadway Hospital was one of the most dreary and depressing-looking buildings in London. It was drab and bare, and such was the state of my mind that everything about it seemed to me to reek of discomfort, illness and death. My heart sank within me when I entered its gaunt portals, ascended in the dark, antiquated lift, and walked down the long corridors, smelling unpleasantly of polish and antiseptic. A large nurse with an Australian accent took my name and led me to my room. There were two beds, two bedside tables, a cupboard and a wash-basin. My sister said good-bye and the door shut behind her—I could almost say 'clanged' behind her, for I could not escape from the feeling that this was my cell where I was to serve an indefinite sentence of imprisonment.

CHAPTER IX

THE man in the neighbouring bed was screened off, but by the noises coming from behind the screens I could tell he was being washed by a nurse. Meanwhile the Australian girl helped me to undress and arranged my washing utensils and my books beside me on my bedside table. She was kind and amiable, but like most nurses in English hospitals, she seemed afraid of deviating from the stony-faced, impersonal detachment, of which our nursing profession seems to be so proud. This was my first experience of a civilian hospital. I wondered then, as I have continued to wonder ever since, what was gained by making a hospital more like a penitentiary for the reformation of convicts than an institution for the care of the sick.

The other nurse finished washing my companion and removed the screens. He appeared to be a boy of about seventeen. He told me later that his name was Bert Tuttle, and that he was waiting for a major operation. I discovered in the course of time that he had been in bed, critically ill, for about three years. At one stage his case had been so hopeless that the hospital would no longer keep him; then, at home, a miracle had taken place; he had started to get better and better until at last he was re-admitted to the Broadway for an operation which, if successful, would restore him to a condition in which he could lead a comparatively normal, sheltered life.

The Sister in charge of our ward, a very pleasant and good-natured Irish lady, came to see me. She told me that I would have to spend a month completely relaxed—so completely I would not even be allowed to wash myself, and certainly I must never leave my bed. At the end of the month some decision would be taken as to what was the best form of active treatment for me to undergo.

96

Bert had a wireless and had developed an interest in good music, which was fortunate for me as we listened in to nearly every broadcast concert. Less fortunately, he was keenly interested in all the B.B.C.'s weekly variety shows, in which the same antiquated jokes are flogged unmercifully, presented this way and that way, disguised but never altered, whilst an instructed audience of sycophants obliges with a constant guffaw of background merriment and many a burst of handclapping.

I realised immediately that I must waste this spell of enforced idleness as little as possible, so I endeavoured to arrange my day into periods of reading. I had always wanted to read through all Plato's dialogues, and this seemed an excellent opportunity; also, history was a useful and absorbing subject to study. For lighter literature I selected all the Somerset Maugham novels which I had not had the opportunity of reading before.

I was in the private wing of the hospital, so I was allowed to have visitors every afternoon as well as for a short while in the evening.

Dermot O'Malley had come home from the Balkans the previous summer to sit an examination which would make him a permanent member of the Foreign Service. He had failed; partly, I think, because the life no longer appealed to him now that he had had experience of it. To my amazement, and I think to the amazement of all his other friends, he announced that his intention was to take up farming. In my own mind, I thought that three months on a farm would be sufficient to drive him back to the froth and glamour of a more social life. But as the months wore on he seemed more and more delighted with his new occupation. He approached farming scientifically via the textbooks, but, at the same time, from the intensely practical aspect, because he took a job as a pupil on a large farm and gradually worked his way through all the most menial and arduous tasks. It was impossible to imagine Dermot rising at five o'clock in the morning to milk the cows; Dermot on hands and knees scrubbing the stables; Dermot, fascinated and happy, ploughing a field. I still pictured him, debonair, charming, and always so immaculately dressed, clasping a cocktail glass, whilst the brittle, insipid conversation bubbled around him.

Mrs. O'Malley had an idea that Dermot's dead brother had insinuated the will, the desire, and the inspiration into his mind. The brother who had been so different, and whose one ambition in life was to possess and to work his own farm. It was certain that Dermot had discovered happiness and fulfilment out of an existence which was wholly divorced from his own distinctive *métier*. Also, it proved undeniable that he was receiving a miraculous aid from some hidden source, which was enabling him to assimilate all the intricacies of farming just as if it had been his one absorbing interest from his early childhood. During the next few years it became demonstrably clear that Dermot did not aspire to be a gentleman-farmer; instead, he entered enthusiastically into the toil and grind of small-scale farming, eventually on a farm of his own, and, what is more, when he pitted himself in competition with those who were able to bring to bear a lifetime of knowledge and experience, he justified himself and won their unbounded respect.

The windows of our room looked out on a rather squalid little back alleyway, on the far side of which was the Nurses' Home—a bare, uniform, red-brick building. I could see just a tiny patch of sky—enough to judge whether the day was fine or cloudy. I often reflected on the grim reality of those lines from Oscar Wilde's 'Ballad of Reading Gaol':

> "I never saw a man who looked
>   With such a wistful eye
>   Upon that little tent of blue
>   Which prisoners call the sky,
>   And at every drifting cloud that went
>   With sails of silver by."

I soon learned that tuberculosis can be the most dreary and tedious disease which man is called upon to undergo. It is true that recovery is possible, but the patient must acclimatise himself to many months of slow, undramatic, scarcely perceptible improvement. The chief problem is how to maintain oneself in good spirits while this lethargic healing process is taking place; it is especially hard for a person who has always been intensely active, both mentally and physically. I took heart from Bert's wonderful courage. He had just left school when he had been diagnosed, at the age of fourteen, and ever since he had conducted an epic, lonely battle. He was, at last, in sight of victory, but what an appalling obstacle separated him from it—three operations which would involve the removal of almost his entire complement of ribs from one side, and the complete closing down of one of his lungs. He was always cheerful; he used to gaze at the little tent of blue for hours at a time, and I imagined he was thinking some unbelievable thoughts as seeing that same sky unfettered by window-frames, and walking over God's fresh fields, surrounded by God's green trees and God's many-coloured flowers.

It is not altogether strange how, during a protracted spell in hospital, every day seems to be endless, and yet in retrospect all the days run into one another, and you look back on one long, unbroken period which might have been a month, a day, or even an hour.

Dr. Baker, my house physician, came and saw me frequently. He was a likeable young man who did his best to keep me optimistic. He firmly believed that a complete and rapid cure for T.B. was almost at hand, and he approached every case with a complete confidence that one of the present methods of treatment would eventually bring about the desired result. Dr. Roberts, the specialist, did his round every Saturday afternoon. He was the master strategist who decided on the moves from time to time, and he left Baker to put them into effect. Baker's visits were informal; he used to sit on my bed discussing the news, books, plays; anything I think, to keep my mind off my disease. On the other hand, Dr. Roberts' round was always the height of formality. He would be followed by a Sister, a nurse, and a flock of junior physicians, but somehow he invariably succeeded, with a few well-chosen words, in reassuring me and persuading me that I was going to get better again.

Generally, I succeeded in keeping myself in good spirits. I was certain that, all in good time, I would rise from my sick-bed and continue the fascinating progress through the unexplored lanes of the future. Occasionally I felt weighed down by depression; at such times I was unable to think of what lay ahead without an agonising sense of the hopelessness of it all. Supposing I did not get well? Would I have the courage to endure the long, weary battle against a death which approached gradually, with a dreadful, unrelenting inevitability? Or, if they partially cured me; it might mean that I would have to see out the rest of my days as a semi-invalid; living and partly living, a bath-chair in the sun, early nights, patent medicines and everybody trying to be nice: "Poor old Tobias, must go and see him again—dreadful strain; never know quite what to say to the poor chap." That black, lurking shadow of abnormality which had dogged me since that misty morning in Holland. I wanted to be the same as other people; I longed to mix with the crowds, unnoticed, to live as they lived, feel as they felt, enjoy as they enjoyed.

Already I noticed how the nurses treated me as one of the outcasts. Very kindly, of course. Usually, very tactfully. But the patients were a different species from themselves. We were tuberculous persons (the word 'consumption' was unpopular in the medical profession). They let things slip out now and then. A nurse bathing me asked me if I was married. "It's a good thing you're not," she said. "Of course you'll never be able to marry now, unless you marry another like yourself." One day another nurse was talking to Bert about Tuberculosis Settlements. "They make you very comfortable; everything is provided, and they look after you very well. Not a bad idea at all for people like you."

When they said things like that; when they looked at me in a certain way; when anything had that meaning or that implication, it was as if a dagger was being driven into my heart and twisted slowly. 'I will show them it's not true,' I thought. 'I will escape from all this—I must escape.'

Whenever I spoke about the future or about my plans, they dropped their eyes and fidgeted uncomfortably. They seemed obsessed with the futility of the struggle. Even Dr. Baker did not let me talk about returning to work.

"Concentrate first on overcoming the disease," he said. "It is useless to waste your energy worrying about what comes after."

One day they painted Bert with iodine and wrapped him up in antiseptic bandages. It was a warm afternoon and he felt hot and uncomfortable. It seemed ages before the theatre orderlies came in, bundled him on to a trolley and took him away; he was terrified out of his wits, but nobody had time to comfort and reassure him. Then nurses came in and made his bed, which was wheeled up to the theatre.

I was taken down for an X-ray. I went in a chair, pushed by an orderly, along endless bare, desolate corridors. It struck me how like a prison was the Broadway Hospital. The staff seemed always to be unhappy; for ever quarrelling with each other. The 'waiting-room' of the X-ray department was a draughty passage, where the orderlies deposited their human cargoes on trolleys and chairs in a long queue. Sometimes you had to wait here for an hour, unattended, before the radiographers were ready to take your film. Nurses and orderlies passed continuously up and down the passage; when they knew you they would half-smile and mumble a few words almost under their breath; it was a breach of hospital discipline for them to show any further recognition.

Bert returned that evening, unconscious, and for the next

101

few days was in great pain. The first stage of his operation, however, proved to be entirely successful.

Fortunately for me, my first cousin was chief assistant to the senior surgeon at the Broadway. He visited me almost every day and always kept me informed about my progress. About this time he told me that Dr. Roberts planned artificially to collapse my bad lung. He explained to me just how this would be done.

Dr. Roberts called in on the Saturday morning. My bed was surrounded by a throng of doctors and nurses. I was told that they did not expect that the artificial collapse could be brought about; if not, it would probably mean an operation. Roberts gave me a local anæsthetic which made my chest feel stiff and heavy. For half an hour he was busy with needles and tubes; no one spoke; then Roberts stood up.

"I think it's successful," he said. "You must lie almost motionless for twenty-four hours."

They all went out.

Bert was eating his lunch; he could not see me because there were screens round my bed.

"O.K.?" he enquired.

"Perfectly," I told him.

He asked me if I'd mind the wireless, so I told him I would like it. Suddenly Delibes' ballet music from *Coppelia* flooded the room. I closed my eyes. The mazurka from the First Act, that incredibly gay, joyful tune. I remembered hearing it once, a long time ago, on leave during the war; I had arrived at the theatre late with a girl friend, and as we had entered the auditorium the *corps de ballet* were dancing that same mazurka—I recalled their flawless grace and precision, and the ecstasy of the audience. At that moment my thoughts took wings and I was drifting timelessly far from the hospital bed, the tubes and the needles. Far away from the physical ugliness of the ward, I was transported by the spiritual beauty of the music and the dance. It is moments like that which made the tedium of a long illness endurable; moments when the soul bursts asunder the thongs which entwine the body, and the patient achieves a freedom and a peacefulness which make worth while everything that he will have to endure in the future.

For days my treatment hung in the balance. My artificial collapse, known by the initials A.P., was the subject of much controversy; Dr. Roberts wanted to leave it—the surgeon wanted to abandon it and operate. Eventually, another specialist was called, and he expressed himself to be in favour of giving it a trial. Throughout this period I was being taken almost daily to the X-ray screening-room, where Dr. Baker scrutinised my chest. Every few days the medical trolley was wheeled into our room by a nurse, who then painted my chest with iodine for Baker to get to work on it with the air-refill apparatus.

Bert went up to the theatre a second and a third time. He withstood his operations and suffered no complications, but it was a terrific ordeal for a boy of his years.

Christmas was approaching. I dreaded the unnatural gaiety, the forced hilarity, to which I guessed we would have to subject ourselves. I had been in hospital for three months and I had been given no indication whatever of how much longer I would stay on until I was within sight of a cure. Christmas to me provided a landmark; something to which I could look forward only inasmuch as it would denote the close of the year in which I had been so ill. Dr. Roberts had had my name accepted on the waiting list of the Hedgely Sanatorium in Sussex. Everybody spoke extremely well of the comfort there and the pleasant atmosphere. I was told it was open to both men and women, and the male patients were mostly ex-servicemen who had contracted their disease during the war or as a result of wounds or imprisonment. Dr. Baker said that it was a rule at Hedgely never to admit any patients who did not stand a very strong chance of being completely cured, as there was some stipulation to that effect in the terms of the sanatorium's endowment regulations. Unfortunately, the waiting list was very long, and I would probably have to remain in the Broadway until the early spring. For the remainder of the winter the thought of Hedgely was a constant source of strength and hope; I longed for the day I would be able to go there.

In the middle of December a grey-haired man moved into the room next door. He was awaiting an operation and was allowed to wander about the floor in his dressing-gown. He sometimes came in to see Bert and me and invariably succeeded in filling us with gloom and despondency as his sole topic of conversation was T.B.

"We're lepers," he used to say. "We'll be lepers for the rest of our lives. People will always avoid us; I notice it already among my friends."

Our special nurse was a delightful and amusing dumpy little Australian, whom we used to call 'Auntie'. She was always a bundle of fun, and was one of the best nurses who has ever looked after me. Nothing was too much trouble for 'Auntie'; she loved London and she used to tell us about the things she did, the theatres, the concerts, the trips, and the sightseeing expeditions. When she talked and when she described her experiences, she seemed to bring her life, her gloriously healthy existence, into the bare, characterless room.

On Christmas Day the doctors and the nurses gave a concert. All the patients had bottles of wine and spirits sent in to them; and then Christmas was over; the specialists returned to their rounds, and the surgeons to their operating tables.

Since my first day at the Broadway I had been keeping a diary. I had never kept one before, and I have never done so since. When I take out the book now and flick over its pages, it brings back vividly the emptiness of those days, and the ever alternating moods of hope and despair. I suppose it assisted in breaking the dreadful monotony, to write down one's thoughts and reactions at the close of each day. It helped too, in some odd way, to give one strength, for, as Oscar Wilde remarked in his intensely moving *De Profundis*: "To become the spectator of one's life is to escape the suffering of life."

On the last day of 1948 I wrote in my diary:

"I have never lost confidence and I will not do so now. I still hope to be cured next summer, and to resume work in the autumn. Even if I must spend a year on my recovery, it will not have been entirely wasted. It has provided an opportunity for coming to terms with myself, and for re-adjusting my outlook towards life."

That night we were kept awake by the singing in the public-house beneath our window, and there were several early morning calls from the Fire Station just down the road.

At the beginning of January, Dr. Roberts told me he was pleased with my progress, and he felt very hopeful concerning my response to the treatment. As a mark of his pleasure I was thenceforth allowed to have two pillows instead of the one on which I had had to lie previously.

I was becoming increasingly exasperated with my long confinement in bed. The pages of my diary for the month of January were filled with gloomy reflections. I often thought about the complete unimportance of material values.

"The penniless tramp trudging the streets," I wrote, "is richer far than the millionaire in a big, luxurious sick-room."

At that time nothing seemed to be so important as good health, and the irony of it all was that anybody, no matter how rich, no matter how brilliant, and no matter how powerful, might suddenly be stricken down with some dreadful disease. Illness was the common denominator of life, the cruel and ruthless leveller of humanity.

From thoughts like these my mind sometimes wandered into other channels. If existence was denuded of all its frills and fineries where did we stand then?

"All beauty belongs to the soul," reflects my diary.

105

"Physical loveliness is very often a mask beneath which is hidden gross ugliness. Conversely, one is sometimes deceived by unthinking physical repulsion into missing a great depth of hidden beauty."

I suppose my generation had been far too cynical. But we grew up between the shadows of two wars. We cherished an insane desire to live, to seize what enjoyment we could whilst there was still time. When I was only thirteen, I and my contemporaries like me were charging across our school playing fields with blunted bayonets; at eighteen, we were charging across training grounds with bayonets sharpened ready for real use. And in our spare time we were lured by the glitter of artificiality—we were going to be to-morrow's 'glorious dead', so we must pack everything we could into our fleeting minutes; experience, worldly wisdom, and scarlet life. It was years later we learned to respect one of the most superb qualities of all—purity, and discovered that the man who is strongest of all is he who is pure of heart.

It was February before Dr. Roberts said:

"Well, Tobias, you can start getting up once a day and walking to the toilet."

My exaltation was unbounded. I longed for the next morning as greatly as I had longed for anything throughout my life. It was not only the thought of leaving my bed and walking; it was the special significance of being permitted to do so; it meant that I had turned the corner and I was now getting better. I had been troubled with sleeplessness at night and this particular night I dozed fitfully, waking up a score of times. I finally awoke at six o'clock the next morning. After breakfast, 'Auntie' escorted me along the passage. It was an exhilarating experience but I felt surprisingly weak and tottery.

Instead of my chart being marked 'Absolute Rest', it was now 'Once a day—toilet'. Bert was ahead of me, for he was 'Sitting up for half an hour a day'. I shall never forget the scene when his mother and father first saw him leave his bed and stagger round the room. They stood and watched, absolutely spell-bound, while tears of sheer joyfulness clouded their eyes.

The winter season of promenade concerts was now over, so that our evenings of entertainment were finished. But there was a new spirit of optimism pervading us both.

It was only a few days after I had first started to get up, that Sister came in and told me there was a vacancy for me at Hedgely, and they wanted me to go down in two days' time. At last things had started to move, I thought. My brother-in-law, Roderick Shackleton, visited me and once again assured me I need have no worries about the future.

"You get yourself cured," he said. "I promise you it will work out all right after that. I will take you for a year as my pupil, and then you will be offered a permanent place in my Chambers."

There was a lot of clearing-up to be done before I went to Hedgely, and I had a number of business letters to write, so my last two days at the Broadway passed very quickly.

I was told that I would have to arrange for some relative to travel with me in the ambulance, and one of my sisters offered to accompany me. We left the hospital after lunch in a very small, one-bed ambulance, which looked like a converted baker's van, but was very comfortable inside. The only drawback was the petrol fumes which seeped in through the back ventilators and eventually made us both feel extremely sick. The journey was an entrancing experience for me. To move down the crowded London streets; to see the people, the shops and the buses. And afterwards, when we had left the city, to speed through the country lanes. I lay back on the stretcher bed, quite fascinated by the greenness of the bushes, the fields, and the trees. The last time I had seen the countryside it had been in the barren senility of the autumn, and I had subconsciously retained that impression in my mind. I was quite surprised to see the luxuriant freshness of the approaching spring. It

107

was as though a magical transformation had occurred overnight.

My sister and I were both wondering how much longer we would have to endure the fumes, and, more important, how much longer we would be able to hold out without actually being sick, when the ambulance pulled up. I looked out of the window and saw a pleasant-looking building, rather like a hotel or a large country club. The ambulance doors were opened, and two smiling porters lifted me out and helped me into a wheel-chair. I was taken to an X-ray room. More smiles and charm. Everyone seemed so nice and so happy it was almost bewildering. Next, one of the porters took me in a lift to the first floor, and then down a long corridor. He threw open a door at the end.

"Well, here's your new home."

The room was small, tidy and newly decorated. It did not look like a hospital bedroom at all. The bed seemed to be an ordinary bed, and the chairs, the dressing-table, and the wardrobe all seemed to be ordinary pieces of bedroom furniture. Most of the outer wall was taken up with a large window which was opened wide. I looked out. A well-kept lawn with two magnificent magnolia trees in the centre. Then a mass of flower-beds stretching away to a thick pine forest. And dominating it all, in the background, the South Downs, looking deceptively near and well-defined in the lukewarm sunshine.

"Well," the porter smiled, "all right for you?"

"Indeed, yes," I said.

"It faces south, too," he told me. "You get the sun in here all day long. Most of the rooms have balconies, and the patients wander around in the warm weather. I'll tell the nurse you've arrived."

He went out. I could not take my eyes off the trees and the hills. It was so tremendously peaceful that I felt an inner upsurging of strength. I knew for a certainty that I had come to a place where I would be immensely happy. Nothing could possibly go wrong in an atmosphere such as

108

this; my treatment would succeed and I would be completely cured.

A nurse brought in my tea on a tray. My sister had returned to London in the ambulance and had not had time to stay, but she was wonderfully impressed by what she had seen.

"I suppose you'd like to be left alone while you have your tea?" the nurse asked.

I assured her that I had so much to ask about Hedgely, that if she had a few minutes to spare I should like her to stay. She told me that this was a slack period during the day, so she could remain with me for five or ten minutes. I plied her with questions which she did her best to answer, although she had only been in the sanatorium for a very short while.

"Why is everyone so nice here?" I asked.

"So you've noticed that already? People always remark on it. I don't know, really. The patients are always very happy, and the staff are very happy too; perhaps it's because we're all treated so considerately—I really can't say. I've worked in a lot of hospitals, but I've never found anything quite like this."

CHAPTER X

HEDGELY was completely self-contained, with its own general stores, post office and barber's shop inside the building. Part of the treatment for the patients consisted of complete freedom, so far as was possible, from all mental worries, and their welfare was planned with elaborate care. The smallest component unit was the 'floor', which consisted of about twenty patients with a Sister in charge. Patients were, of course, in varying stages of recovery, ranging from the completely bedridden to those on the brink of their discharge who were living fairly normal lives. The patients were largely responsible for their own administration; the welfare executive for the floor being the 'floor representative', who had a seat on the Sanatorium General Purposes Committee, and it was his duty to see that all the jobs on the floor were being carried out effectively. These jobs comprised the collection and posting of letters at various times of the day; the morning shopping; taking round morning and evening newspapers; the collection of orders for, and the subsequent delivery of, fruit and flowers; and a whole series of other tasks which provided something useful with which the ambulant patients could occupy themselves, apart from the fact that this made life a good deal pleasanter for those in bed.

The main General Purposes Committee was made up of a chairman, who was the patients' 'head boy', an entertainments secretary, a wireless secretary, a treasurer, and the individual floor representatives. Hedgely had its own internal broadcasting system so that an enterprising entertainments secretary had ample scope for organising what talent was available among the fit patients. It was indeed a happy and well organised little community, and I saw from the start that the spirit of service to one's

110

fellows appeared to be dominant in the minds of all.

Within a few days I had met all the walking patients on my floor. They were men of all ages; a general, a naval captain, and a brigadier at one end of the scale, and an eighteen-year-old schoolboy at the other. But for the most part they were ex-servicemen, about my own age, who had contracted their illness during the recent war; a high percentage had been prisoners either in Germany or in the Far East.

On the medical side there was a meticulous system of gradually increasing exercise for patients whose disease had been stabilised, in order to see if they were fit to withstand the stress and strain of normal life. I was immediately graded 'I.L.O.', which meant that I was allowed to walk once a day to the lavatory. Apart from the luxury of this one visit, I was strictly confined to my bed. I was informed, however, that when one had started to climb the ladder of recuperation, promotion to a higher grade was apt to come regularly every week or two.

There was none of the artificial discipline of an ordinary hospital about Hedgely. As soon as the staff knew a patient sufficiently well they called him by his christian name, a delicate policy which was neither encouraged nor forbidden by the higher authorities, but a practice I may say that I never once saw abused. Both the patients and the staff seemed to be proud of their good-natured, informal relationship, and by unspoken consent everybody did their best, by judgment and common sense, to preserve it unblemished. The Sister in charge of my floor was an Austrian Jewess who was respected and popular with all of us. Probably it was her intelligent understanding of our feelings which gave us such confidence in her, for she had once been a patient at Hedgely herself, and she appreciated the long-drawn mental struggle against doubts and fears which every T.B. sufferer has to overcome before finally becoming rid of the disease.

During my first week or two, when I was still learning

about the methods and administration of Hedgely, I began to wonder increasingly what sort of a man was Dr. Pearce, the Medical Superintendent of the sanatorium. I had been told often that as a specialist he ranked amongst the leading experts in the world, and I accepted that estimation from people in his own profession; what interested me more was his ability for organising our communal existence. Obviously he must be a man of immense personality, for his influence pervaded every minute detail of all our lives. I met him a few days after I arrived. He came into my room on his weekly round, a quiet-voiced, middle-aged Australian, who explained to me shortly and sympathetically just what were my chances of complete recovery. I had an opportunity later of observing him in more detail, and I was to discover that the source of his strength was a kind of aloof independence in conjunction with a complete confidence in his own decisions, and a quite incredibly wide knowledge of human nature. He was always approachable by the very humblest person in Hedgely, and when he was approached he invariably showed himself to be fully aware of every thought and mood which rippled through the sanatorium.

The spring was fine and warm and I gradually found myself being moulded into the peaceful pattern of Hedgely. I knew that I must fight against this mental indolence and physical lethargy, for fear that it might set its permanent stamp on my life. There were many men at the sanatorium who had developed the dulled sensitivity and the feelingless automatism which is so beneficial in the conquest of the tubercle bacilli, but so fatal in ordinary, competitive existence. It was very easy to fall into a frame of mind like that. Everything was found, everything provided; existence endless and timeless. Why should one deliberately struggle back to the careworn ruthless turmoil of normality? Was it not better to spin out an extended lease of life in the sheltered and coddled atmosphere of Hedgely? But quickly I turned away from the suggestion; the sanatorium must only be an interlude. I had come too far to give up. I must overcome this harmful intoxicant. After all, I thought, if I was only seeking a way of escape there would be many other avenues equally attractive.

So I progressed through the grades: 'II.L.O.'—walk to lavatory whenever necessary; 'Bed II'—at liberty to roam about the floor in a dressing-gown. And then 'D'—up for dinner—the thrill of putting on proper clothes for the first time after seven months in pyjamas. But it was an anti-climax when I arrived downstairs in the lounges and the large dining-hall. The conversation was endless T.B., gossip about the staff; gossip about other patients; gossip about the various forms of treatment. T.B., T.B., and more T.B. In that narrow little world ideas and thoughts seemed utterly circumscribed. After dinner people wandered around list-lessly; everything seemed so futile and aimless. I discovered that for many of them their sheltered isolation had built up a shadowy fear of the outside world, and they did not really want to go back. This was particularly noticeable among the women and the girls. I noticed that consumption seemed to stalk the globe with eyes of a sadistic cupid, for the victims it sought to enslave were usually the youngest and the fairest and the most beautiful. The disease often heightened their prettiness.

There was no segregation of the sexes at Hedgely. Dr. Pearce, with his usual foresight, realised that the flirtations and romances which were always taking place among the patients meant as little as the affairs on board ship, and usually swept along their gay course—and on to a premature conclusion. Very occasionally, couples did get married after they had left the sanatorium, but far more frequently these friendships eventually found their way into the participants' dimmed alcoves of harmless, hidden memories.

When I was getting up to tea and dinner I was asked to take over the appointment of Chairman of the patients' committee. I accepted with pleasure, both because I was feeling the need of something to occupy my attention, and also because I wished to delve more deeply into the mind and methods of Dr. Pearce, the central figure in our parochial life. The Chairman was the liaison officer between the Medical Superintendent and the patients on all matters of administration; his job was to ensure that all submerged grievances were exposed and demolished before they could disrupt the congenial happiness which was such an essential feature of Hedgely.

The committee at that time was a forceful one. The Entertainments Secretary was fruitful in ideas, and his originality was ably supported by his assistants. The Secretary was a personal friend of mine and so was the Treasurer, so we could work amicably together. I had been asked to write a mock murder trial for broadcasting to the bed patients. In fact, when it was put on, the cast all dressed up for their parts, and the 'studio audience' of staff and patients received the performance with good-natured indulgence. I think the actors derived a fair amount of enjoyment out of their preparations, and certainly for me, as the anxious producer, it assisted admirably in passing the time. Then there was the quarterly magazine to produce; this was undertaken by an Anglo-Catholic priest, assisted by a very erudite young lady who had recently taken an honours degree in philosophy. I suddenly found myself fairly preoccupied and contented. The most important thing of all was that my promotion from grade to grade was being achieved with consistent regularity, and the doctors were even enquiring when it would suit me best to recommence my work.

The routine of our lives was restful and easy. The day started with the night-nurse bringing a cup of tea to every bedroom at about seven o'clock in the morning. Patients took their own temperatures, and filled in their own temperature charts. There was sometimes rather a scrimmage for the limited number of bathrooms, but I discovered that by rising fairly early I could bath and shave at my ease. Breakfast, for those fortunate enough to be up for the whole day, was served at half-past eight. After

breakfast the bed patients waited for their letters and newspapers; people who were dressed were divided between
those who had to return to their rooms to rest, and the
more advanced grades who had to take a walk of a prescribed distance.

At midday electric gongs sounded throughout the building for the first rest-hour. During the ensuing period every
patient was obliged to recline on his bed. You were
allowed to read or to listen to the wireless, but talking or
writing were forbidden. At one o'clock the gongs sounded
again and people who were up to lunch made their way to
the dining-hall. At half-past two some went out walking,
others once more returned to their rooms until tea-time.

The second compulsory rest-hour was from half-past five
until half-past six in the evening.

At this time there was a vogue for farewell cocktail-
parties. It was strictly against the rules to bring any
alcoholic drink into the sanatorium; not because it would
interfere with the treatment, but because the temptations
of indiscriminate drinking might prove irresistible among
people enduring the boredom of that extremely indolent
existence. Anyhow, it was becoming the custom for
patients on the eve of their discharge to hold secret cocktail-
parties to which they invited all their friends and acquaintances. The time was always the same, immediately after
the evening rest-hour. So on a party night you would see
a general movement towards one of the small lounges.
Once inside, glasses were produced from pocket or hand-
bag and for the next half-hour, until the dinner gong
sounded, men and women indulged themselves in the
fanciful gaiety of the free and healthy. Perhaps I was not
the only one who was struck by the relentless irony which
electrified the atmosphere on these occasions. Even when
patients simulated the thoughtless flippancies of habitual
cocktail-party conversation, it became blatantly obvious
that their illness, and all the mental anguish and physical
suffering it had involved, had taught them a far greater

115

depth of truth than was known to the people whom they endeavoured to mimic. It is the universal law that once anyone has walked in the shadow of death, he will ever-more hear the echoes of laughter through the vaults of sadness.

And so in due course, as the summer wore on, I was allowed to get up for lunch and eventually for breakfast. Even then I was not at liberty to wander in the beautiful gardens; however, I was allowed to sit out in one of the alcoves built into a wall, enmeshed with copious strands of wistaria. There we used to sit and read and have endless discussions about life.

One day a friend and I took a taxi to a neighbouring village and had lunch at a charming little public-house. We both felt, when we sat in the bar, as though we had been out of England for a long time and we avidly listened to hear what the people were saying to one another. We wondered whether we would ever again be able to feel as they felt, or to talk as they were talking, because our lives seemed to have deviated so much from theirs. When we drove back through the sanatorium gates it seemed as if we were entering once more into our voluntary prison.

I used to have doubts sometimes as to whether I would ever be able to put up with the wear and tear, the hustle and bustle, of my career as a barrister. I had become so lazy. It was always being drummed into us that we must rest. "Rest is the principal weapon against the bacilli"; "Never stand up when you can sit down"; "If you have nothing to do, lie down on your bed"; "Do not worry about anything, because worry brings on the disease". My mind was gradually becoming attuned to a state of non-reality. The only logical thing to do after this indoctrination was to go off and live in a monastery. What would it seem like to be plunged straight back into the harshness of cut-throat, competitive life after this prolonged course of deliberate softening up?

I was always very interested to observe other people's

reactions to illness and disablement, and as I wandered from room to room visiting the bedridden I often discussed with them their psychological reactions to their condition. Up to a point the feeling was universal: the devastating shock when the disease was diagnosed had given way to the gradual realisation that a slow, wasting death was by no means an inevitability; the struggle to re-orientate oneself to a new life; the swiftly alternating moods of blissful optimism and of black despair. But beyond that point everyone was different; no two people can possibly face disaster with identical philosophies, or even with the same degree of faith and constancy. It was necessary for all of us, as we passed through those seemingly endless, wearying hours lying on our backs, to puzzle out what we really believed about ourselves and about creation as a whole; every individual reached his own conclusions, and I discovered that the people who seemed most satisfied were those who turned for solace and comfort to the teachings of Christianity, or, alternatively, those who were driven by disbelief into a fatalistic agnosticism.

I noticed too that tuberculosis seemed to awaken in its victims an intense craving for all the beauty of life, coupled with a fervent desire for self-expression. Many who had never put brush to paper in their lives now turned to art, and I was told there was a remarkably high standard among the patients. It was impossible to find amongst these artists any common characteristic of personality or outlook. On my floor a naval captain, a town-planning officer, and a tailor were all passionate devotees and all confessed to me that the idea of painting had never crossed their minds before this. I did not take it up myself and I was frequently mystified by the apparent ease with which a person, quite late in life, could dip into the hidden recesses of his mind, to reproduce some dimly-remembered landscape which had taken his fancy in bygone years.

A pastime which I could understand and share was the enjoyment of music. Here again, a lot of people had quite

117

suddenly started to listen to concerts and grown ardently enthusiastic. There were a score of rooms in which one would always be welcome if one went in to discuss last evening's 'prom' or some favourite composer or concerto.

And there were, of course, the people who lay doing nothing, taking no interest, only cursing the fate which had brought them to this pass, and for ever speculating about the state of their lungs and their chances for the future.

Eventually I was put on the final grading of all—'Exercise'. First of all you had to pass a half-mile test. I took my first walk after a breakfast on a very hot day. It was laid down that you rested for half an hour on your bed, then a nurse noted your pulse-rate and your temperature. Your guide, another patient who had previously negotiated the test, led you out of the front door and on to the drive. The distance was carefully measured; you followed the drive to the quarter-mile post, and turned to retrace your steps, keeping an eye on your watch; the permitted time was between twelve and fifteen minutes. People approached their tests with an odd mixture of excitement and anxiety. One had come so far on the road to recovery, it seemed, that this was the crucial moment which was to decide whether one would be able to bear the exquisite burden of ordinary living. It was a thrilling experience to be walking, with the fields and the trees on either side, and the sky, no longer a little tent of blue, but now a vast celestial dome, dipping on one side into the distant hills and on the other into a luxuriant pine forest.

As I walked, I thought of the tests we had taken in the Army, not so many years previously. Six miles in one hour and ten miles in two hours, marching and doubling alternately, carrying a rifle and full equipment. It was a bit different now, but it seemed just as much of an achievement if one could get through it.

When we reached the sanatorium again, my guide said: "Not bad, twelve minutes."

Back in my room I lay on my bed. Temperature and

pulse on return, again after five minutes, again after half an hour. The doctor looked at the figures and told me I had passed. At lunch people offered their congratulations; it was as if I had been promoted to the sixth form. As a matter of fact there was something of a school-form atmosphere about the medical grades. There was a tendency to cluster in your own group: the 'exercise' people had little to do with the 'lunch, tea and dinner' contingent, and anyone on 'tea and dinner' felt himself distinctly superior to a person on 'dinner only'. This was, I suppose, a natural reaction to progressive grading. As well as that, it had its roots in the camaraderie of fellow-travellers; those who have traversed all the laps of the journey together, faced all its hazards and overcome all its obstacles in conjunction, do not look outside their own company for comradeship. The present was always in the hands of the people on 'exercise'; the future rested on the up-and-coming in the ranks of the 'dinner only's'.

From then on I could take my daily half-mile walk with my friends after breakfast, free from the strain and anguish of tests, pulse-readings, and temperature charts. Sometimes we used to wander far beyond the prescribed span, for we were allowed to choose our own routes, and we would pause a while in some attractive clearing, to sit and talk and, for those who wished, to smoke a leisurely cigarette. Then we would stroll home and disperse to our rooms, where our letters and newspapers would have been left on our beds.

Before patients went away from the sanatorium they were permitted to take a forty-eight-hour leave. This was principally to accustom them to the outside world. Some people told me that when the time arrived to leave the sheltered seclusion of this pampered existence, patients were filled with awe, and a large number wished to remain where they were. There were stories, too, about the extreme difficulty of settling down to normal life, the constant uncertainty about one's condition and the perpetual hankering to escape from it all and to return to the aimless and amiable tranquillity of Hedgely. I listened to these tales without any misgivings; I had already experienced the lonely personal combat of rehabilitation, those uncertain and clutching moments when crutches are taken away from you and you are forced to mingle with the heartless, jostling crowd. This would be easier than last time because I knew what to expect; above all, I knew that you have only to be patient, and you will be gradually merged into the throng until you become one of them. In time, the cruellest scars will lose their crimson ferocity and become a faded white line, pale and scarcely perceptible. One of the most thoughtful ideas of the Creator was to make man so immensely adáptable.

I did not apply for a forty-eight-hour pass, but I went out a couple more times to lunch and tea, and occasionally some of us would hire a car and drive to a near-by park to watch a game of polo.

I was beginning to waste more and more time. My powers of concentration seemed to be diminishing; no longer did I fill my reading hours with a carefully planned time-table. First of all I discovered that I was reading my legal text-books mechanically, without assimilating anything I read, so I put them aside. It was the same with philosophy and history; then I grew listless with novels. Finally I could not even muster up the mental energy to work through *The Times*, my daily newspaper. During the compulsory rest-hour I turned on the wireless and almost counted the minutes until I could leave my bed and wander around again. I enquired among my friends and I found that my experience was pretty general.

A lot of very active people are fond of saying that, if they were faced with a long illness, they would read and study, or write novels or memoirs. I wonder if they realise how deadening is the effect of a long confinement. When you are leading a busy life you employ your leisure to the full, but when all your time is leisure, then you lose that vital zest without which the mind goes dull and flat, and the flow of inspiration becomes a feeble trickle.

At the end of July I was given my 'Date'. Dr. Pearce, on his weekly round, pulled out his diary and told me I could be discharged after the August Bank Holiday. We settled the day and he made a note of it. There was not much for me to arrange; my brother-in-law, Roderick Shackleton, and my elder sister had just taken a country house where he could relax at week-ends and during the vacation, because his practice at the Bar was becoming so busy. They invited me to spend the summer with them, until I was allowed to commence working. My sister offered to come down to Hedgely and collect me in her car.

I called a meeting of the committee to hand over my job as Chairman, and started a long round of farewell visits. It was as though I had come to the end of a long voyage. I felt no regrets and no excitement; once again I seemed to see myself from a slight distance, as though I was watching a play. All this was written; all ordained. At moments like this, time lost its meaning and all its importance. If I closed my eyes, allowing my imagination full scope, I was almost transferred from the present into the future, and all I was doing appeared to have happened in the past—that strange feeling that things are moving in continuous, repetitive cycles, or, perhaps, that your life is in other hands than your own, and you are permitted odd impersonal glimpses before you step back into your body, leaving the audience to take up your position in the centre of the stage.

As sanatorium beds were so limited in this country, Hedgely discharged its patients before they were fully convalesced. Usually the amount of exercise on which they passed one out was a mile walk every morning and either half a mile or a mile again in the afternoon. I had been doing the full distance for a week when I was given my date, and I felt extraordinarily well. Everyone had a final interview with Dr. Pearce, at which they learned the characteristics of their particular case, and he gave them advice and guidance for the future. He explained to me, that in my particular form of treatment the cure would not be completed for four or five years, during which time I would have to continue paying weekly visits to hospital in order that more air might be pumped into my chest; I would also be obliged to take things fairly easy, lying down for an hour every day and going to bed early at night. All this would be relatively simple to carry out, but one thing that caused me a sharp pang of regret was the condition that I must never sunbathe—this was an inviolable rule. I thought of the exquisite feeling of lying in trunks on the beach on a hot day and letting the heat of the sun seep into your flesh.

"Most dangerous for you," said the doctor.

He then told me I could get back to work after two months, but for one month I was to work mornings only, and then gradually build up normal daily hours.

"Can you do this?" he enquired.

"I can," I said, "but it may be difficult."

"It is always difficult," he remarked cryptically. "Anyhow, it's for you to choose between giving yourself a decent chance to make a complete recovery, or returning to Hedgely in a year or two's time."

He shrugged: "Of course, your treatment hasn't been too satisfactory, mechanically. You should get away with it, always remembering the ever-present element of bad luck."

The day before I was to leave I had arranged to give a farewell party together with two other men and a girl who were being discharged the same week. Our combined invitation list totalled between forty and fifty, so the small lounge would be filled to capacity. Our bottles of gin and sherry were brought to the sanatorium by the fiancé of one of the female patients, a man who was staying at a hotel in the village. He entered into his task of gin-running in a thoroughly conspiratorial way and went to extreme lengths to camouflage his parcels. When we made our last-minute computations, we decided that we needed one more bottle. Somebody phoned the fiancé and he promised to get it. I was standing in the entrance hall at lunch-time, when it was always crowded with doctors, nurses and patients; suddenly the fiancé rushed in the front door, came straight across to me and shoved a brown paper parcel into my hands.

"Your football boots," he announced proudly, in his loudest voice, with an obvious wink which contorted half his face.

Several members of the staff near-by eyed my parcel with suspicious eyes, but nobody asked any questions.

Just before lunch I had a telephone message from my younger sister.

"I'm afraid I've got very bad news," she said. "Roderick collapsed yesterday in the High Court. He's in a Nursing Home, unconscious."

"He's been overworking," I said. "He needs a good rest."

"It's far worse than that. The doctors say he won't come round again—it's a matter of hours."

Roderick died that day. My other sister, his widow, asked me to come and stay with her still. I hesitated, but she said I would be doing her a kindness as she could not bear to be by herself at that moment. Eventually I agreed to spend a few days at home in London, and then to stay with her in the country for a month or so.

I told my close friends what had occurred, and they persuaded me to carry on, at any rate nominally, as one of the hosts at the party. I compromised by just going into the lounge to wish everyone good-bye.

The following day my sister drove me away from the sanatorium, down the long winding drive and out of the main gates.

CHAPTER XI

SEBASTIAN SHAW had been for many years Roderick's closest friend. He was a barrister, and some people prophesied that he would end up a High Court Judge; he was a Member of Parliament, and some prophesied that he would finish as a Cabinet Minister. His dominant characteristic was his great personal charm, and coupled with this he was a skilful raconteur; he was also witty, amusing, and fairly popular.

Sebastian was at that time in the middle forties, and looked absurdly young for his age. I had known him intermittently for a long time. I should say that I had technically known him for, in fact, I had not really known him at all. He was one of those men with whom it is easy to be at all times on light friendship, but extremely difficult to know with any degree of intimacy.

As soon as Roderick died, Sebastian invited me to become his pupil for a year. I agreed willingly; for one thing, he was in Roderick's Chambers; for another, I knew that Roderick would have liked me to go with him. Sebastian had the perfect practice from a pupil's point of view—plenty of work and a wide range of variety. I knew and regretted that the chance of a lifetime had gone, as I had been told very often that Roderick was a brilliant master who took infinite care over his pupils, and loved to pass on to others his encyclopædic knowledge of the law and his superb skill as a tactician. At times there had seemed no limits to the heights to which he would have risen, except to the very few people who knew that he was always fighting against an incurable internal complaint, an illness which had become more and more out of hand until, at the end, he was staving off death with one hand each time he put on his wig and gown to take part in a case. And

124

that was how his shadow eventually overtook him—on his way into the Courts, which he loved as much as I have ever known any man to love his occupation, with his brief in his hand, and his mind filled with the lucid arguments he would propound on behalf of his client.

Names fade as quickly at the Bar as they do in any other walk of life. Roderick's name remained on the door outside his Chambers, and on the board at the bottom of the stairs, but he himself quickly became one of the nameless ghosts of the past. He had not had time to place himself on the stands of immortality, so his reputation was soon remembered only by a handful of his closest associates. Roderick had always been an uncomplaining realist, and he would have known perfectly well that it would happen like that. So be it.

Sebastian disliked teaching, and I knew this. He had had one pupil once, and had vowed he would never have another. I mentioned this to him.

"It's different with you," he said. "And anyhow I do it for Roderick's sake. I owe him a good deal. He got me into these Chambers after the war—he has always helped in a number of ways besides that. I suppose I shall now be an unwilling legatee of most of his practice."

He asked me how I felt physically. I assured him I was perfectly fit.

"Of course you won't practise yourself? You'll take a settled job after this year with me, won't you?" he asked.

"I intend to practise," I told him.

"Then I think you're foolish. There are many well-paid, easy jobs for men who have given up the Bar."

"For men who have tried the Bar and failed?" I suggested.

"Yes—I admit that—but after all your case is different." The Bar is a harsh task-master. Even if you're a hundred per cent fit, with no incapacities, it is terribly hard going. You'd better face the truth now, no matter how brutal it may be. You'll always worry about your voice; admittedly you speak very well, but you are still a bit hesitant, and you still stumble over words from time to time. It is an impossible handicap in our profession, and it will be bound to get you down sooner or later. Even apart from your voice you have so many other things wrong with you. I don't want to discourage you, but after all you have been called to the Bar—you have made the gesture."

"I never intended to make a gesture," I said.

"What then?" he asked.

I did not know what to reply. Perhaps I had not yet sorted out my motives to my own satisfaction; perhaps I was afraid that any analysis might only serve to expose a blind obstinacy.

"I'd prefer to see how things go," I said.

That was the truth, but only half the truth. I had developed an uncompromising faith in the future. I felt that everything somehow would turn out for the best. I preferred to fight now, as I had been forced to fight ever since that shell in Holland. I was leaning all the time as I had often been told to lean and His mercy would provide.

Sebastian stuck to his argument.

"It's obviously idiotic for someone with your health to be ambitious."

"But I am not ambitious at all."

"Then," he said triumphantly, "that only proves my point. The Bar is a career only for the ambitious."

I wondered how I could make him understand, with his searching and logical brain, that there were an infinity of driving forces in life, of which the lust for worldly success was only one. It seemed impossible to explain to anybody who had not spent long months in illness or in captivity the perfect joy of moving unnoticed in crowds and doing the things they are doing, or the bliss of being able to lose yourself in your surroundings so that all becomes immutable, painless and eternal.

I only wanted to fulfil my cherished wish of following my chosen career, that was all. I wanted to work beside my colleagues, amidst all the vicissitudes of their profes-

126

sional life; to suffer their setbacks and share their successes until, at last, I was accepted as one of themselves, and not just as a person making an ephemeral 'gesture'. And surely even the selfish test of achievement was the procurement of happiness? And happiness was by no means dependent on earthly things. The ambitious man will never be contented, for there is no ceiling to success. It was making a dreadful travesty out of life, to consider that you were wasting your time if you did not manage to grind your way forward in front of your fellow men.

I felt I was doing right while I was following a harmless occupation which would keep me happy, and besides, if you deviate from the path which is intended for you there comes an indescribable, though quite unmistakable, warning; a tuneless discord in the system, which is in vivid contrast with the natural harmony which comes when you are following the authorised route of your destiny. If I felt that warning I would immediately alter my plans.

The real question for someone like myself was how was one going to treat one's disability. I was convinced by that time that the Creator did not wish the disabled to scuttle to the nearest foxhole, but to meet the challenge with His assistance. It was essentially a personal experiment with a theory, which I would have to see out to its final conclusion. I had gone so far, and every step I trod convinced me of the truth of what I believed.

Sebastian said: "Well, anyhow, don't worry about it. I'll do everything I can to make you happy while you're with me, and I hope we'll get on well together."

I had to visit the Broadway Hospital every Wednesday afternoon for my refill of air. Normally, the public clinics were grossly overcrowded, but I had the good fortune of being invited to join a very small clinic, normally reserved for doctors and nurses with T.B. This meant that I could avoid hours of queueing in the cheerless waiting-hall of the Broadway. Usually there were only three or four of us, and in time we became very friendly. I often wondered how I would be able to observe regular attendances when I became even moderately busy at the Bar. It seemed impossible to say: "I will never do any work on a Wednesday afternoon." If you accepted a brief, you often had no idea of the date on which the case would be heard before the Courts. Worse still, what would happen if I was appearing in a case which was in full swing at the time of the clinic? The only solution—an absurdly impossible one—would be for me to rise just before the luncheon adjournment, and say to the judge:

"If your lordship pleases, it would be highly inconvenient for me to appear before your lordship this afternoon, as I have to report for out-patient treatment at a hospital. The nature of the treatment is such that if I was to delay even until to-morrow, the result might well be disastrous."

The judge would be sympathetic; he would be helpful, but it would be a wholly unfair request. He would have to consider the expense, the inconvenience, and many other things; for instance, the police, witnesses and jurymen who would be affected. It would certainly cross his mind that, as things were, I should not be endeavouring to practise as a barrister.

I shelved this problem along with many others. Some solution would probably turn up in good time.

I enjoyed my two months of convalescence before I started work. I felt fresh and eager, and every hour of the day was full of enchantment. In hospital I had sometimes been assailed by a whimsical longing to see again incongruous and unaccountable things. At one time I wanted to look at a London street at night after a shower of rain, all even and polished and reflecting the light from the lamps; another time, a farmer's dog driving a small herd of cattle —seen from a distant hill, so that all was still except for a rustle of movement, and all was quiet except for the dog's staccato barking and an occasional grunt from the farmer himself; and a public-house the moment you enter from the darkness outside; the sounds, the people, and the brightness, and nobody turning to stare at you. These and a host of other things I was now seeing again, and I was revelling in the fullness of life.

It was satisfying to notice how little everything had altered. Each day I was observing small incidents which I had half remembered, half forgotten, and I was thinking: 'I belong here; this is my world.' In the place from which I had just come everything worked according to its own rules, and I had felt continually out of place; but here all was rational, and I seemed to know what was to happen the fraction of a second before it actually occurred.

And then the day came when I was allowed to begin working. I travelled on the Underground from South Kensington to the Temple, along with the girls from government offices, smart, sophisticated and detached, who poured from the train at St. James's Park and Westminster; other barristers were there with their black hats, rolled umbrellas and brief-cases; at first sight they were difficult to pick out from the immaculate gentlemen on their way to the City, but I learned quickly to recognise the latter, because they always seemed more prosperous and less worried, and they frequently carried a copy of the day's *Financial Times*—a certain mark of identification.

I left the train at the Temple station, joined the throng hurrying along the Embankment, and turned with them to pass through the gates at the bottom of Middle Temple Lane. I had looked forward to this moment for years—the moment when I would enter into the Temple, my Temple, on my way to my own Chambers. But I did not feel at all possessive that morning. I felt instead a mood of intense humility. This little kingdom was ageless and inviolable; it was founded on centuries of tradition and unassailed principles. The buildings, the lanes, and the courtyards were filled with the past, so that the whole atmosphere became timeless, and in every corner crouched some great figure of the bygone days—or some figure from the myriad of nonentities who once trod so briskly where I was treading now, and in after years had retreated bowed and broken, to turn his back on the citadel for ever. The whole of the Temple is saturated with history, and a newcomer feels constantly that the ghosts of former generations are watching, and listening with critical attention, to see that their jealously guarded precedents are in no way upset.

As I walked into Chambers, I was struck by the air of tranquillity and peace, for I had not yet discovered that the Temple retains a quiet dignity even during its own modest rush-hour. Sebastian's rooms were on the top of the block, at the head of a steep flight of narrow stone steps. These were only temporary Chambers until some of the new buildings were finished, as the German bombers, with their unhappy knack of striking down the antique and the beautiful, had cast a trail of chaos and destruction over this tiny, pacific sector of the capital. The head of these Chambers was a venerable old man, well on in the seventies, who looked as though he had stepped straight out of a volume of Dickens. He found the stairs very heavy going at his age and, indeed, the only time he was seen by the pupils was when mounting them laboriously, or pausing for breath, a white-haired, Pickwickian figure who was always courteous and chatty, even though he did not know you from Adam. It was generally appreciated that he was only a very nominal head of Chambers; Roderick had been the senior junior, and his place was now taken by a brilliant little Scotsman. But the really effective figure in all deliberations affecting the Chambers was the senior clerk, George. George had been there throughout the war and was acknowledged to be one of the most efficient clerks in the Temple, and he was certainly one of the busiest, for he had utilised the war years to sow the seeds for the future, and had amassed such a flow of work that all his barristers were kept constantly dashing from Court to Court, which was good for them and remunerative for George as he worked on a commission basis, retaining a set percentage of all the fees which came in.

There were six barristers in the Chambers, together with six pupils, three clerks, and three secretaries. The atmosphere was an extremely friendly and happy one.

George also had some sort of connection with the set of Chambers below our own, which were equally busy and prosperous, and he used to interchange work between the two. The pupils were permitted to do their own cases if they were lucky enough to get any, and George would sometimes hand out work to his particular favourites among them.

Sometimes one of my fellow pupils would take George for a drink at a near-by public-house. On these occasions George, his tongue loosened no doubt, would ruminate on the life of the Temple.

"I can make or break any of you," he would say affably.

But George, even if he had had the inclination, certainly had not the time to devote to career-wrecking. Almost every minute of the day was spent in furthering the interests of his Chambers. And money was pouring in, thanks to the efficiency of George and the ability of his barristers. So they all had every reason to be contented.

Once, in a mood of whimsy, George was supposed to have told someone that he felt half-inclined to read for the Bar himself.

"When I see the standard of some of the people who are coming along nowadays," he said, "I feel strongly tempted."

The pupils had their own room. They were all men about my own years who had served in the forces during the war, which made us all well above the average age at which barristers normally pass through their pupillage. Sebastian and Gordon Lomax shared a room which was joined to ours by a connecting door. They had both been in Roderick's own Chambers before the war, but as all the members had joined up, Roderick had been obliged to close the set down in 1939. When he had been invalided out of the Army a year before the war ended, Roderick was invited to join the present set of Chambers, with the

131

intention that when the elderly head eventually retired, there would be a sufficiently able and experienced man to take over his work. Roderick consented to this offer, on condition that places would be found for Sebastian and Gordon when they were demobilised in due course.

The position of a pupil at the Bar is a strange one. He pays his 'master', the barrister to whom he becomes attached, a fee for six months or a year. He is then at liberty to open any of the master's papers, and write out his own opinions, notes, pleadings and advices. He can also accompany his master into Court, and sit beside him in wig and gown when he does a case.

Sebastian had two other pupils. One finished shortly after I arrived and I did not ever get to know him properly; the other had only started his pupillage a few months previously, so we did the main part of our term together. I liked Robin from the first time we met, and a friendship sprang up between us which persisted undiminished even after our ways had separated. He was a first-class scholar and possessed an immense knowledge of the law, even at the outset of his career. He had had a good war, seeing plenty of fighting, and being decorated for bravery. After his release from the Army he went up to Cambridge and won various academic laurels. Roderick had always said that he considered a pupil a burden for the first six months and an asset for the last six, but Robin commenced turning out accomplished opinions directly he started, and Sebastian soon realised that he was going to be worth his weight in gold.

Robin's great hobby was politics. He was an ardent and devoted worker for the Conservative cause, and spent many evenings lecturing or addressing meetings on their behalf. I often envied his tremendous energy, above all else his ability to work with a clear and lucid brain until well after midnight, following a long day of arduous work.

There was a strong clash of political views in the pupils' room, with Robin on the right and Karl, who had spent much of his early life in Austria, on the left. And then there was Edgar, a fanatical Communist who always carried his *Daily Worker* respectably concealed inside a copy of *The Times*. However, there were not many political discussions as the pervading impression was principally one of incessant hard work.

Across the way, where the secretaries had their rooms, there did not exist the same atmosphere of studious intensity, and the busy chattering of typewriters was interrupted spasmodically by piercing screams, giggles, and animated scuffling. These sounds belonged to a different planet, and the earnest pupils, with a common, long-suffering tact, closed their ears, and buried themselves even deeper in their papers, manuals and law reports.

These secretaries were a delightful lot of girls, all hand-picked by the indomitable George. We had a shrewd suspicion that the chief quality which he had looked for at their preliminary interviews had been their pleasing looks. Certainly it was true they were as efficient as they were attractive, but that may have been a tribute to George's luck rather than his judgment. He was very proud of his girls, and watched over them with the protective eyes of a jealous father. They could hurt him easily by not paying him enough attention, and he rewarded them kindly and thoughtfully with prolonged holidays and extra days off duty. It was noticeable that the various barristers who had engaged and were paying the girls had little or no say in their affairs. It had become an established rule that they were 'George's young ladies'.

I enjoyed the work I was doing immensely. I used to arrive just before ten each morning, and choose a set of papers from Sebastian's desk. On the days when he was not in Court it was possible to take one's time over preparing whatever the solicitors had asked for. We had a sizeable library in Chambers, and it was possible, if necessary, to go over to our respective Inns of Court libraries for a more detailed authority. It was customary

133

for a pupil, when he had finished his draft, to fold it up with the papers and to return them to his master's table. In due course, when the master was ready to tackle the work himself, the pupil would sit in his room and they would discuss the case together. Sometimes a pupil's work was adopted in whole, sometimes in part, and of course on other occasions it found its way by a speedy and direct route into the waste-paper basket.

When Sebastian was in Court in and around London, Robin and I would accompany him, to take notes and prepare references. After the case we would enter into a lively discussion on its conduct and its merits. Very often we crossed the road to the High Court of Justice to spend a morning doing three or four undefended divorces. We would then sit in Court waiting until our cases were called, or listening to the brief formalities with which a marriage tie could be so easily terminated.

But underlying the hollow ritual there was always something far deeper and more moving; it only required a flicker of imagination, when a husband or a wife petitioner was giving the unhappy story from the witness box, to bring the picture to life in all its frustration and misery. I often reflected rather sadly how quickly love and affection could turn into hatred and bitterness. A divorce suit which was defended was an even more painful performance, for then the whole of the miserable married life came under the spotlight, with all its secrets and all its intimacies. The two aspirants would sit on opposite sides of the Court, surrounded by their followers, and they would pass into the box in turn, to chronicle the other party's defects and blemishes. It was strange, at such moments, to reflect that on a certain day, which they both may have then thought to be the happiest of their lives, they had stood together, while their friends, those two factions who now glared at each other across the room, had poured forth their lavish compliments and congratulations. Robin used to shake his head and tell me it undermined his faith in marriage, but apparently the damage was by no means irreparable, because within a comparatively short time he announced his own engagement.

One became *blasé* very quickly, for it is impossible to run through the gamut of emotions every day. In the first divorce, the first breach of contract, the first negligence action, the first criminal charge, the characters are real and alive in all their novelty; you move when they move; you experience what they had experienced; you follow the course of the trial with the passions of a partisan. Later, the whole thing becomes far more impersonal, which is a very good thing, as it is only from a position of slightly distant detachment that one can form true and fair opinions. Doctors and surgeons must have the same experience; in the beginning they are dealing with people first and cases second, but it is only a matter of time before the case takes precedence over the person.

In Chambers we lived law and talked law. Even at lunch in the Inn, seated on benches at long tables under the lofty, hammer-beam roof of the stately hall, we met our friends, and they discussed their cases with us and we discussed our cases with them. There is a custom in Temple which is sacrosanct—that when you are consulted by a colleague on a professional matter, you must give him the full benefits of your knowledge and experience. I first learned this in the pupils' room, for no matter how busy a person was, if you raised a point that was causing you trouble, he would lay aside his work and explore all the possibilities as keenly as though the problem were his own. I discovered later how this practice is in the very life-blood of the Bar. When I, at length, received my first set of papers, Sebastian and Gordon asked me to come in and tell them about the case; they both put away what they were doing and discussed my case with me for over half an hour. But this is only one of the incidents of the wonderful camaraderie that exists among barristers. It is not a mere historical formula which requires a counsel in Court to refer to his opponent as 'my learned friend', or more simply as 'my friend', it is also a token of the brotherhood in which they are bound. The traditions of the Bar allow no member to address another as 'sir', or to ever use the prefix 'mister'. When the lowest is addressing the highest, he simply calls him by his surname.

I often wish the people who are so fond of alluding to the sharp practices and underhand methods of lawyers in general could know something of the standards of professional honour and dignity which at the Bar are cherished with such pride and held in such reverence that they have grown into the very symbols of all that is greatest in the still unsullied conception of British Justice.

My only regret, at that time, was that I was obliged to finish work at lunch-time. I could not help a slight feeling of guilt as I used to leave the Temple around two o'clock. Successful men have never tired of pointing out that the way to success is by hard work. Robin certainly deserved to be successful by this criterion, I thought, for, not content with his day's work, he would take home more sets of papers to browse over in the evening. But I had two sides to my life, and they seemed to be always pulling against one another. I was in no doubt which one must triumph. I must obviously adapt my ways according to the dictates of my health, for it would be no good to chase off in the pursuit of laurels if that road would lead straight back to a hospital bed. It was ridiculous, I realised, but the thought was ever there, and I could not help wondering whether those who did not understand my peculiar circumstances considered me a slacker and a backslider. I knew the other pupils were sympathetic, but that did not help, as I was certain, at the same time, they thought me foolish to set myself such a difficult task. At times someone made a vague suggestion about a sheltered job in a Ministry, and I wondered whether these kind fellows were aware that they were only sharpening my determination to see this thing through.

Apart from a tendency to tire quickly I was perfectly fit. I rested as much as possible, and went to bed ridiculously early at night. After all, it was not as though this molly-coddling was going to be permanent. In four years' time, or maybe five, I would be as active as the best of them, and already the months were flicking by. Soon I was allowed to work one afternoon a week, then two afternoons, then three. I felt better; I was really making progress at last. This was a more normal life.

CHAPTER XII

THERE had been a time when the Bar was a career only for the young man who was aristocratic, privileged and wealthy. This was no longer the case. Most of my contemporaries had turned aside the chance of comfortable incomes, an assured future, and the stalwart foundation of security, and had elected to plunge themselves into the vortex of life at the Temple, which seemed at times to offer to the faithful only frustration, bankruptcy and ruin. A few were well-off, some possessed small private incomes, the majority had only what they earned by the sweat of their brows. So it was a case of lecturing night after night, marking papers for correspondence schools, scribbling articles for the legal journals—there were many recognised ways of earning the modest income that would provide the economic possibility to carry on. There was always a large pool of highly-trained, intelligent men for any employer who offered spare-time evening work, and in consequence most of these employers drove a ruthless bargain. It was a fact that graduates with the highest academic qualifications were toiling at a lower rate per hour than the Temple cleaners, the good women who dust, sweep and scrub before the day's work commences. However, it was all accepted without a murmur: this was part of the life; they did their damnedest to break you, and only the fittest survived.

If the very junior Bar had a motto it would be: 'Hang on!' That was the thought in the back of everybody's mind in the early days. But there was an echo which always whispered: 'Can I?' It had been bad for years, and now it was worse than ever, because an influx of ex-servicemen was swamping the market. As well as the normal quota who would have qualified every year, we had the impatient, restless, precipitate throng, piled up from six years of war. On top of that, the Temple had been blitzed. The buildings were not there; the Chambers were not there; the chances were not there and the work was not there. Obviously a lot of people would have to abandon it and give the others breathing space. Soon they would start drifting away to the well-paid jobs, it was said, and then—but who would start the rot?

"I wonder who will be the first of our lot to give up?" pondered one of my friends at lunch, and each one of us thought: 'Not I.'

Sometimes I used to look round the pupils' room and wonder which of them would be the big names of the future. By the window sat Desmond, an ex-Guards officer. He was one of those who could afford to wait, for although he was a married man with a child, he had sufficient wealth to live in comparative luxury. He was a happy soul and always courteous and charming.

Karl was also married, but his position was a very different one. He had embarked on a frenzied two years, and he told us frankly that if he could not make ends meet by the end of that time he would be forced to give up.

"Not for myself," he said, "I could stick it out, but my wife and baby—it is for them."

Edgar shared my table, which was not a very good thing, as he smoked endlessly and I seemed to work in a permanent nicotine haze. I had not the heart to tell him how I loathed it, for he had a fidgety, nervous disposition, and I knew he needed his cigarettes as much as I needed my fresh air. Edgar looked like a young Stafford Cripps, with his thin, pale face and thoughtful eyes behind his horn-rimmed spectacles. He was an idealist and a fanatic. He had the passionate humanitarianism of every sincere idealist and the bitter acrimony of every devout fanatic. But we all liked him, and I often thought how much more kind and sympathetic he was in his personal relationships than in his political viewpoint.

Robin was eager for success. At that moment the only way he could show his industry was by his insatiable appetite for hard work. He was usually the first pupil to arrive in the morning, and always the last to leave at night. So far in his life, hard work had provided him with the key to most doors. His father had had very little money in the early days, and Robin himself had passed through his public school and university education on exhibitions and scholar-ships. .

Lastly there was Godfrey, a pleasant-natured South African, who was returning to his own country at the end of his pupillage. Perhaps it would not be unfair to Godfrey to say that he took life a little more lightly than the rest of us, but he was considerably younger, and he was a very good games player.

Gradually I met others in different Chambers. I saw the same rugged determination everywhere, the same dangling crisis overhanging every life, and the same unwillingness ever to admit the possibility of defeat. They were all so different, and yet they all had one thing in common, the same burning conviction that the Bar was for them the only possible career.

There was one man whose personality greatly took my fancy. Tall, sturdy, and good-looking, he had been a para-trooper during the war. A few years back he had had an excellent job in commerce, but he had been discontented with it; he had been troubled constantly with an urge to throw it up and to try the life at the Bar for which he had always yearned. Eventually, when he was almost forty, he had made up his mind, and once his mind was made up there was no turning back. He read for the Bar in his spare time, and immediately on being called he resigned his position.

"It's been tough going," he told me, "with a wife and three kids, but it will come out all right—it's simply got to."

We used to stroll in the Temple gardens for ten minutes after lunch.

"It is so difficult," he said once, "when nobody has any faith in you except yourself. I don't blame my wife, I know it's been damned hard on her. We've all had to give up a lot. And, what's more, she knows I could go back to a well-paid job in commerce to-morrow if I wanted to. But I never will. This is the life." He stopped suddenly and struck his clenched right fist into his open left hand: "I'm not going out of this until somebody pushes me out," he muttered angrily.

The one problem all our pupils had to face was the seemingly hopeless task of finding Chambers at the end of their year. It was common knowledge that at the outset of your career the type of Chambers you joined largely decided whether you would get away to a flying start or be ground down into obscurity. It was comparatively easy to secure a place in one of those briefless sets of Chambers which are littered profusely throughout the Temple. They would always welcome you as one more person to share the rent and their other financial burdens. In return, your name would go up on the door and your address would appear in the Law List, but you would have to face the soul-destroying monotony of a barren desk and a future which would be inevitably foredoomed. On the other hand, those who were lucky enough to secure a place in some busy Chambers found a constant supply of work passing down to them from the people above, and if they were any good at all they very soon began to acquire solicitor clients of their own.

Theoretically, a pupil was supposed either to be taken on in his pupil Chambers as a tenant, otherwise the senior clerk in normal times was meant to find him a place elsewhere. Nobody had been absorbed into our Chambers since immediately after the war when Roderick had arranged for one of his pupils to stay on. George always promised every pupil that he would try to find him a set of first-class Chambers at the end of his year, but somehow these never materialised. Of course it was extremely difficult at that time, and it usually required weeks or months of dogged searching before a pupil eventually found himself somewhere to go.

Karl's time expired soon after I arrived, and he started his unenviable quest.

One morning he seemed to be in the depths of despair. I was sitting alone with him in our room.

"You have no idea what it is like," he said bitterly. "I think I must have canvassed half the Chambers in the Temple. It is always the same—all full up—all have some-one who's been promised the next vacancy. I feel just like an unemployed tramp looking for a job, trailing round hat in hand. I suppose," he added thoughtfully, "that it is much the same experience being a door-to-door salesman. 'Not to-day,' every time as the door is slammed in your face."

It must have been extra-difficult for Karl, as we all knew he was very able and only required the right opening to go forging ahead.

"I'm glad for your sake you'll be spared all this, Toby," he said. "It wouldn't do your health much good."

"How do you mean, I'll be spared it?"

"Because you're going to stay on here as a tenant, at least that's what everybody believes."

In time Karl found a good opening through a friend of his, and he succeeded in making an incredibly good start. Desmond was the next to go. He did not have to wait for long, because he had the proper connections and the appro-priate influence was brought to bear on his behalf. Then it was Edgar's turn, and his left-wing friends, of whom there were many in the Temple, were ready to lend a helping hand, so in due course a satisfactory place was found for him.

George had decided that there were to be no more pupils after the present contingent had left, so we were getting no regular replacements. Just before Christmas Godfrey returned to South Africa, and it looked as if Robin and I were going to be left alone. But the little Scotsman who was 'number two' in Chambers was getting such a deluge of cases that he was obliged to take another pupil to help him keep abreast of his paper work.

Reginald, who joined us for this purpose, was an Old Etonian, and had already completed a pupillage at the Chancery Bar, where a completely different branch of the law is dealt with. He was in the middle thirties and had previously held some sort of a job in the City. Robin and I found him a delightful companion—good-humoured and very modest—and he had good cause to be proud of himself as he was intellectually brilliant, and further, he had distinguished himself during the war by enlisting as a private soldier and rising to the rank of lieutenant-colonel.

It was a mild winter that year, and now the grass was beginning to freshen in the Inner and Middle Temple gardens, and the trees along the Embankment were stirring themselves with a newly-discovered lease of life.

Robin, Reginald, and I were experiencing the alternations of optimism and depression which are part and parcel of a barrister's life. When I was walking into Chambers in the morning, I used to wonder whether there would be anything for me on my table. It was so easy to half-close your eyes and picture the piles of neat oblong bundles tied up with a single or a double band of red tape, and inscribed on the front: 'Mr. Tobias to advise', 'Case for Mr. Tobias's opinion', 'Brief for Plaintiff', 'Brief for Respondent'. I would check myself abruptly when I was passing the relics of the gutted Inner Temple Hall. This was mere fanciful day-dreaming, but perhaps there was one set of papers, one solitary set with my own name on it. I immediately quickened my pace. Then the stairs; then the clerk's room. George in his shirt-sleeves, with a pencil thrust behind one ear; three telephones ringing at once, a pile of briefs on the desk, stacks of briefs on the mantelpiece. Would he ask me to hurry away to some outlying Court? But no. He looks up as he catches hold of the nearest receiver.

143

"Hulloa—yes—George speaking," then a quick glance at me and a brisk acknowledgement:

"Good-morning, sir."

"Good-morning, George."

I leave the clerk's room and climb a further flight of stairs. Of course George had been busy, as always. Suppose he had forgotten to tell me? There might still be something for me in the pupils' room. I push open the door, and staring me in the face is my own table, bare and unadorned. A blotter, an ink-bottle, a pen-stand, but no papers. And Robin feverishly scribbling one of Sebastian's opinions, with his table littered with open volumes of law reports.

After lunch the paratrooper would say: "It will come. It will come in the end if you stick to it. The only quality worth having in this game is guts."

Four of us made up a 'mess' for a Grand Night dinner in Hall. There are only a few of these dinners each year, and there are usually so many applicants for tickets that you have to draw lots for them. This time we were all lucky.

The ritual for dining in Hall is governed by centuries of custom. The dinner takes place at the usual long tables, and all messes number only four people, who sit two on one side, two on the other, facing each other across the table. The positions in which each member of the mess shall sit is prescribed according to his seniority, and the one who has been longest called to the Bar is automatically the captain of the mess. It is laid down that no member is permitted to talk to a member of another mess, which means, probably, that you are not allowed to speak to the person seated by your side. Captains of neighbouring messes may exchange formal words with each other when necessary, but this relaxation is principally permitted so that requests may be made for essential commodities, such as salt, to be passed along the table.

We all met in a public-house in Fleet Street before the dinner. After having a drink we wandered down to Hall.

It was not customary for the ordinary members to wear evening dress; they were supposed to dine wearing a gown over a dark lounge suit. Hall looked massive and tremendously impressive, with the clusters of orange-tinted lights throwing dark shadows on the magnificent oak roof high overhead. We felt possessive and proud of its stateliness and its antiquity, for we all remembered being told as students that it had been built in 1572. We walked down the long lines of tables, on which the silver glittered over the unblemished purity of the large white tablecloths, and bottles of champagne, bedecked in black and gold, stood evenly spaced like so many toy-town sentries.

The room was filling, and from every side came the hum of conversation and the quickened atmosphere of scarcely suppressed excitement and expectancy.

"Take your places, please!"

The cry was taken up. The fours collected themselves and formed up in their messes. We all stood up as the senior porter, with mace held erect, led in the Benchers and the distinguished guests. They filed past us in twos, each Bencher escorting a guest. It was indeed an imposing array, for those in the procession wore full evening dress with orders and decorations. The Benchers were all judges, judicial officers and eminent barristers, and the guests, led by Her Majesty the Queen, included foreign Ambassadors, Cabinet Ministers, Chiefs of the three fighting Services, Bishops, and a host of other celebrities. They took their places at the top table, which, hundreds of years ago, was given to the Benchers by Queen Elizabeth and at which she was said to have signed the death-warrant of Mary, Queen of Scots. They were separated from the rank and file by another historical table made from the timbers of Sir Francis Drake's ship, the *Golden Hind*, at which, by ancient privilege, only the most senior members who are dining may sit.

It was surprising how effectively the mess system worked. You became completely oblivious of anyone else at the table, and it might well have been that we were the only four in Hall. We drank together, served each other with food in turns, and when the Loving Cup came down to us, as each one stood and drank, another two jumped up and watched over him to guard him from a surprise attack, according to the custom of a bygone age.

The occupants of the top table filed out at the end of the meal, to retire to the Benchers' rooms for dessert. We stayed for a long while talking. Suddenly we noticed that the room was only a third full. Then we piled into a taxi, which did a circular tour, depositing each member of the mess at a railway station or at his home.

Somehow, we all felt that from then onwards our membership of the Inn was fuller and closer, for we had inscribed our names on one of the manifold pages of its august history.

Robin and I found Sebastian a very pleasant master. He had a quick and nimble brain, and he never became so absorbed in his work as to lose sight of the underlying humour of a situation. In time, I realised that he had a remarkable knack of being polite and charming automatically, at a time when his mind was far away. Often he would be sitting at his desk gazing dreamily out of the window, but he was never wasting his time. Indeed, Sebastian never wasted a moment; in reality he would be thrashing out a problem; weighing up arguments and considering a multitude of possibilities.

One morning he called me in to discuss a difficult opinion with him. We had been debating the matter for some time when Gordon—his Scottish room-mate—arrived. Now Gordon was a great radio fan and listened regularly to almost every variety show which was broadcast. That morning he was eager to repeat some of the jokes of the previous evening. He sat down and proceeded to tell Sebastian a succession of amusing stories. I glanced at Sebastian and I could see that he had not the slightest idea of what Gordon was talking about, but from time to time he burst out:

"I say, that's good—very funny indeed—isn't it, Toby?"

He was all smiling attention and convulsed with laughter at just the right moments.

Sometimes Sebastian was vague, but never in any matters that were at all important. One had to get used to recognising whether or not he was really listening.

On one occasion a secretary from Chambers was getting married on a Saturday afternoon. Sebastian had intended to go to the wedding, but at the last moment he was obliged to go off on some constituency business. He asked me particularly to let him know all about it. When I reached Chambers the following Monday I went to his room.

"Good-morning, Toby," he said beaming.

"I went to the wedding," I said.

"Oh, did you?" He looked interested. "How did it go off?"

I briefly described the reception.

"I'm so glad it was so successful," he said warmly.

I turned to go.

"Oh, Toby," he said suddenly.

"Yes?"

"You never told me who was being married, did you?"

I saw immediately that he had only listened with half his attention. I glanced down and noticed some papers open on his desk. I understood.

In the spring we threw open the windows of the pupils' room. Far below in the garden men were cutting the grass and tending the flowers.

Occasionally a young barrister would stroll across the lawns, very thoughtful and very briefless, his black suit looking strangely incongruous against such a floral background. It always seemed still and peaceful, in spite of the constant distant rumbling of the trams on the Embankment.

Robin laid down his pen, and blotted his 'Advice on Evidence'.

"I wonder whether I should do the Statement of Claim

147

in that swimming-bath case, or write my political speech for this evening." he pondered.

He pulled out his calendar and thumbed through the pages.

"Six more weeks," he said thoughtfully, "and my pupillage ends. I suppose I should start looking for Chambers."

I suggested that he should see Sebastian to find out if he had any ideas.

"That's a good scheme," he said. "I'll do it now."

He went through the connecting door, and I left them undisturbed for half an hour. When Robin came back he sat down in his chair.

"Well?" I enquired.

"Toby, I ought to tell you this. I hope it won't put your own plans out. Sebastian has invited me to stay on in these Chambers. I feel a bit awkward on account of you—but we did discuss you too."

"Oh, what did you decide about me?"

"Well, Sebastian feels awfully sorry for you, but he thinks it would be madness for you to keep on at the Bar. He says you'd never stand up to the physical strain of the life—and your voice; it's all right now, but he's certain that it would let you down as soon as you put any serious strain on it. He wants you to get a quiet job somewhere. Would you feel very hurt if I were to become a tenant here, as I know Roderick had wanted you to stay on?"

I assured him I did not mind at all. This had come as no surprise, as I had never shared in the general belief that a place in Chambers was being kept for me. Roderick was dead now and his plans had died with him. If I had learnt one lesson from life, it was that the going is up-hill all the way, and I was not expecting it ever to be otherwise. But something would turn up—something always turns up if one has faith. It was no good worrying about it.

I offered Robin my congratulations.

"That's very nice of you," he said. "Somehow I had felt

rather bad about it. I suppose you'll take Sebastian's advice and look for a job?"

"No," I told him. "When my time finishes I'm going to try and find myself other Chambers."

Perhaps, earlier on, my objective had merely been to qualify in order to prove to others as well as to myself that my brain injury had in no way impaired my faculties. Or perhaps it had been the mere afterglow of a boyhood ambition, fostered by paintings of many generations of ancestors in wig and gown. Now, however, it was something more. Through the half-open door I had glimpsed the path which I knew I must follow, the way I wished to tread, for that was where happiness and fulfilment lay.

Give it all up? I thought of a court-room before the judge entered in the morning. The dry scent from the wooden benches. The clerk busily scribbling; stony-faced warders making their last-minute adjustments; the waiting jurors looking rather dubious, rather lost; counsel filling up their places, poring over their briefs and whispering to the solicitors who were sitting just behind them; and in the public gallery men and women peering forward expectantly. There was the same hushed tensity which electrifies a theatre the very moment before the curtain rises on an eagerly awaited play, and the same brittle, tremulous atmosphere which edges over the concert-hall when the orchestra is tuning up with wildly thrilling discords before the conductor takes his place on the platform. And then, when the first case is called, the flurry of combat, the clash of personalities, the stern struggle for mastery before the inscrutable, ever-watchful faces of the jury. Here they dealt with people and with life, ordinary people at one, perhaps the only one, extraordinary moment of their lives, when they had come into conflict with ruthless, unflinching rules of social conduct. Here were eloquence, drama, emotion, tragedy, and, above all, humanity. No, I would never give it up, for it was in such a setting that the restlessness in my nature had found substitutes for the muddied excitements

149

of a rugby pitch and the hard-earned thrills of a Thames regatta day.

Sebastian was always discovering at the last moment that a case of his was coming up in the High Court. Then he would grab his hat and race down the steps from Chambers. Eventually we had a drill worked out for these occasions. Robin would seize all the necessary papers and books, and the junior clerk would follow with Sebastian's robe-bag. At one stage we were straggled out along King's Bench Walk, Sebastian, head down, moving at a pace something between a walk and a trot, then Robin quite unashamedly running, arms full of a motley assortment of briefs and authorities, then the clerk striding out with his load, and last of all myself, forbidden to hurry or to carry anything heavy. We used to link up in the robing-room at the Courts. As often as not we would then find we had to hang around for half an hour until our case was reached in the list. After that, a coffee and discussion in the refreshment room. It was indeed a pleasant life if one could only escape the uncertainty about finding suitable Chambers in the future.

As Sebastian did not refer to his offer again, Robin approached him after a few weeks had gone by. He came back to the pupils' room looking terribly disappointed.

"Apparently I got it wrong," he told me. "Now Sebastian says that I can stay on rent-free doing his paper-work, but I will not become a member of the Chambers at present and my name will not go up on the door."

I asked him whether he would be absorbed in due course, and he told me Sebastian had been rather vague about that, but had told Robin he would do his best to see he became a member whenever the propitious moment arrived.

"Did you agree?"

"No, it would be madness. There's only one thing for it; I'll have to begin my search for new Chambers straight away."

He went down to speak to George, who told him not to worry. He, George, would find him just the right place.

From then on Robin hawked round, just as Karl had done, and with just as little result. Everywhere it was the same. 'Full up, but why don't you try so-and-so's Chambers?' References and cross-references and the dreary trudge continued.

Then in desperation Robin asked Sebastian to find out from all his friends whether they knew of a vacancy anywhere, and Sebastian promised to do this, but at the same time he renewed his invitation on the same terms as previously.

"Don't you know anyone else?" I asked.

"Only one person." He mentioned the name of an eminent figure in legal circles who had been a great friend of Roderick's, and incidentally had arranged Robin's pupillage with him.

"Why don't you go and see him?"

"It's so awkward," Robin replied. "I don't want to appeal to him unless all else fails—still, it's a last resort that I'll probably have to take sooner or later."

Eventually he wrote a letter. An interview was arranged, and within a week Robin was a member of another set of Chambers.

And then it was my turn. I saw George.

"Yes, sir. I'm perfectly aware your time's nearly up. I've got you in mind; of course I have. But I won't let you go just anywhere. No, nothing but the best. You can rely on me. After all, I was your brother-in-law's clerk."

I thanked him and went to Sebastian. It was the first time we had discussed my future since the afternoon just before I became his pupil.

"My dear fellow," said Sebastian, "I'm glad you've come for a chat. Let's go outside."

He gathered his bowler hat off the peg and we went out together. It was a pleasantly warm, rather sleepy, afternoon and we wandered up to the top of the garden. Then Sebastian stopped:

"It isn't easy to say what I have to say." He looked away

at a large hydrangea. "Toby, you're one of the people to whom we all owe a large debt; a debt we cannot possibly repay. Perhaps you'd find more happiness if you accepted your physical limitations. There's your voice; it's an awful handicap—your hesitancy of speech—you've never had to put it to a real test yet, and I don't think you ever should do so. This business is difficult enough without any disabilities, but with all you have to contend with it's a virtual impossibility. There's your head and chest wounds and your arm—this is no career for you. What chance will you have where only the fittest survive?"

"If I find it too much for me, I can always clear out," I said.

"There's another thing," he went on, "and it's not very pleasant. No head of any other Chambers will take you in if his senior clerk objects. You probably don't know how it usually works. The head of Chambers enquires whether his clerk's agreeable, and the clerk straightaway goes round to see George. 'What sort of a man is Mr. Tobias?' he asks; and George may say: 'He's all right; he would be good if it wasn't for his health, but that is terribly uncertain.' To put it bluntly, from a clerk's point of view you are not a good bet."

"I'm only wasting your time, Sebastian," I said quietly. "I have borne all that in mind and I want to take the chance."

"In that case I shan't try to persuade you differently. Until you find Chambers you can stay on in my room without paying rent, and help me. I'll do all I possibly can to find you a place somewhere. But I still think you shouldn't make up your mind without giving the matter very careful thought. Why not go away for a few weeks' holiday and think it over?"

I had been working for almost a year, and so a holiday was not at all a bad idea. Before I left I spent a few weeks Chamber-hunting. All my fears were only too fully realised. It was Karl's experience and Robin's all over

again—the only openings led straight down blind alley-
ways. All my friends did what they could to help, but
unfortunately most of them were the junior members of
their own sets, without any voice in important Chambers
business.

One of the chief drawbacks of the medical treatment
which I was receiving was that it was vital to obtain my air
refill on a set day each week. In time, you became used to
the methods of the doctor who treated you and, what was
more important, he became accustomed to the delicate
peculiarities of your own individual lung-collapse.

I abhorred the thought of being tied to London for
another five years, so I started to make enquiries about the
possibility of getting refills on the Continent. First of all I
tried Austria, but the Broadway Hospital informed me that
they had no information about the facilities there. Eventually I decided on France and Switzerland; so, armed with a
chart showing my normal air intake and lung pressures, I
set off for the Alps. I had been supplied with a list of all
the clinics and private doctors who could give me this
highly specialised treatment, and it was simply a case of
being in the right town on the right day.

Everything worked out excellently, although there were
several fairly tense moments. Once, in a little mountain
town, I found that the doctor could not speak a word of
English, and my French was decidedly rusty at that time. I
managed to explain my requirements to him, and he told
me to remove my shirt and lie on his table. He had a
couple of assistants and a nurse with him, who all talked
incessantly. Then he called for silence and drove the needle
into my chest. Four heads craned forward. He connected
up the air-tube and the pressure gauge.

"*Maintenant*," he beamed down at me as the air commenced running through.

Two or three minutes later he made a remark to the
others, and immediately they all began to jabber at once. I
was suddenly aware that they were asking me questions,

153

each trying to shout louder than the rest. It seemed desperately important; they were excited and agitated; I looked at the doctor; he was shaking his head wildly and beads of perspiration were glistening on his forehead. In that moment of confusion my comprehension of the French language completely forsook me. I closed my eyes and hoped for the best. A moment later the shouting was stilled and there was a sudden hush. The doctor wiped his brow and pulled out the needle. They all gathered around smiling and congratulating me. I do not know to this day what was the trouble.

CHAPTER XIII

I COULD understand Sebastian's gloomy outlook about my future. It is difficult for anyone to comprehend how others can cope with disabilities from which they do not suffer themselves. Even now, when my right leg has fully recovered, I am lost in wonderment as to how a lame person can try to live an ordinary life. But there are ways of overcoming all incapacities and when it is necessary, indeed vital, some method is usually available.

Soon after I had been wounded I had noticed a strange fact. In this country physical disabilities are always treated with respect; most people are willing to help the limbless or the cripple. Other afflictions, however, fail to meet with a similar sympathetic response. For instance, deafness and defects of speech. No comedian would joke about the hardships endured by a one-legged man, but the terrible isolation of deafness and the agonising torments of the stutterer are fair game for the music-hall stage. As well as that, in the realms of social intercourse these two misfortunes, instead of arousing pity, seem to evoke only either badinage or irritability. I think I suffered more embarrassment with my speech than with anything else. In the early days it was a considerable effort to say anything, because I had to work out my exact words beforehand and rehearse them in my mind. Then, in a moment when there was a lull in the conversation, I would blurt them out, stammer and trip in my confusion, and once more recede into silence. I used to dread going into a shop, buying a bus ticket, even answering the telephone, and I was all the time aware that my nervousness was making it even more difficult. Supposing, I thought, supposing I just did not care; if I only could remain quite calm and unperturbed when I was speaking. I started to devote an hour every day to reading

155

aloud to myself in the privacy of my bedroom. I kept this up for years until the terrors of speaking gradually disappeared.

When I returned to Chambers nothing had developed; nothing altered. I resumed my dreary quest until I was dreaming at night of mounting endless, sharp, stone steps that led to nowhere. I had moved into the room which Sebastian shared with Gordon, and everything seemed to be settling down with the aspect of permanency.

Eventually, in desperation, I remembered Mr. Justice Tremayne, who had signed my papers before I had been called to the Bar. I thought of his words: 'If you are in any trouble come and see me.' I wrote him a letter. The following day his clerk came round to see me with a note from the judge, suggesting that I should call on him for a chat one morning before he went into Court.

When I was shown into his room, he was writing at his desk. Immediately he jumped up, smiling, and shook me by the hand. We sat down in arm-chairs by a blazing coal-fire, and he asked me about various members of my family whom he knew. Then he stood up and walked over to the window.

"Well, Toby—what's the trouble: Chambers, is it?"

I told him how my greatest efforts to find a place had had no result.

"I had always assumed you would stay on in your present set. Would you like to?"

"No, Judge. Not now."

"I see," he said. "I think I understand how it is."

I asked him if he thought I was foolish to keep on wanting to practise at the Bar.

"Why ever not?" he exclaimed.

"My voice."

"There's nothing at all the matter with it," he said emphatically. "If you think this is the life for you, you should stick it out no matter what happens and despite what anyone says to you."

156

"Even if you had told me it was no good going **on,** I wouldn't have believed you, Judge," I remarked.

"I should think not, too," he replied. "Well ,Toby, I'm glad you came to me. I only regret you didn't come earlier. Don't worry about looking for Chambers; I think I can find some for you."

He asked me how the different members of pupil Chambers were getting on, and we chatted for half an hour until his clerk came in.

"Excuse me, sir," he said, "but it's time to robe."

"Oh, dear," the judge said laughingly. "I have a most tricky judgment to deliver presently. I'm sure the Court of Appeal will tear it to pieces."

He showed me out to the door and placed a hand on my shoulder:

"Everything will turn out all right in the end, Toby, so don't worry yourself."

I mumbled something meaningless. I did not really know what to say, for my gratitude and my admiration were beyond any words I could speak.

A week later the judge rang me up.

"Do you know Clarence Jupiter?" he asked.

I replied that I had never met him, but of course I knew him by name, for Jupiter was a famous K.C.

"Well, go and see him now. If he likes you he'll take you into his Chambers."

I hurried round immediately. The senior clerk, Percy, told me that Clarence Jupiter had just gone over to the High Court, but he had left a message for me to come and see him that evening; meanwhile he wanted me to have a talk with his clerk.

"Just so that I can give you the low-down on what it's like here," said Percy.

I told him right away that I had been shot up rather badly during the war: "I want you to know this," I said, "so that if you feel the vacancy should go to someone absolutely fit, you can tell me now and I'll understand perfectly."

"We knew all about that, sir," he replied. "If Mr. Jupiter wants you to join us, I certainly wouldn't raise any objections; in fact, we'd all welcome you here, if I may say so, and I intend to do everything I can to assist you. We're a happy lot of Chambers, and I'm sure you'll like the other gentlemen here."

We discussed rent, Chambers' expenses, and clerks' fees, but Percy did not seem particularly interested in his own pocket.

Later that day I saw Clarence Jupiter. He was a dignified, middle-aged man, with a great presence and an alert, un-ruffled manner. He told me he would be pleased to have me in his Chambers and I could start there as soon as I liked. I went back and told George.

"Well," he said, "I'm glad to know we've managed to fix you up at last. But I won't say 'Good-bye' because we'll see a lot more of you in the future."

"When?" I asked, making no effort to conceal my surprise.

"You don't think I'd be unfaithful to Mr. Roderick Shackleton's memory, do you? I'm going to look after you, sir. There's lots of work passing through my hands, as you know full well." He stood up excitedly: "I'll keep you well supplied, sir. I'll send you brief after brief, lots and lots of 'em." He waved his hands wildly above his head, as though he was clutching at invisible briefs which were falling all round him with the profusion of hailstones. "Yes, I'll look after you, you know me, sir. I never make promises which I don't intend to keep."

I thanked him politely, and I could not help wondering vaguely what could be the cause of my sudden popularity. Anyway, I bade him good-night and went on my way down the stairs. I was overtaken by Michael, who had joined the Chambers just after the war. He asked me if I had found a place yet, and I told him my news. He seemed to be delighted.

I walked with him as far as his car, and before climbing

in he said: "Toby, I owed everything to Roderick. I know you'd have stayed on with us if he'd lived. I just want you to understand that I haven't completely forgotten all he did for me. I've made my views quite clear and I'm not the only one either. I'm desperately sorry you're not staying with us. All I can say is 'Good-bye and good luck and I hope you'll show 'em'."

CHAPTER XIV

FOR most people life is divided between sharply contrasting cycles. Sometimes everything we touch turns to laughter and gladness; but at other times we cannot handle anything except it turns to tears and sorrow. I suppose one learns in due course not to be too complacent during the former periods, and not to be too dejected during the latter, for the phases usually follow on each other in fairly strict rotation.

I had a feeling that I would find happiness in Clarence Jupiter's Chambers. I fondly imagined I was like a ship which has glided suddenly from the turmoil and confusion of a stormy ocean into the protected peacefulness of a sheltered harbour.

I liked the large room into which they put my desk. I liked the blazing coal-fire in the spacious hearth, and the shelves of dusty volumes on every wall. I liked the broad open windows facing on to King's Bench Walk. The clerks were obliging and helpful, and the other members of Chambers charming and kind. And my name went up on the door, and my address passed into the official records.

For a moment I could relax; then it struck me—I was feeling ill. I quickly put the idea out of my mind. I was tired, admittedly, and the past months had been a considerable worry, but that was all over now. I had Chambers, good Chambers; everything would go forward smoothly with all the omens favourably inclined. It was undeniable, nevertheless, that certain things were happening inside me which it was difficult to ignore. But it must not be, it could not possibly be. So I threw myself into my work and I played 'let's pretend' with my health.

A few weeks later I could go on bluffing myself no longer. I rang up the Broadway Hospital and they told me to come round immediately. I knew I was running a temperature and had been doing so for days past. It was late in the evening when I arrived at the hospital. The duty physician met me and took me to the X-ray room. As he peered at my chest through the screen, he asked me about my symptoms.

"Yes," he said eventually. "You've got some fluid on the lung. An attack of pleuritis; it shouldn't be serious though. Go home to bed and rest for two days, then come back and see me before you begin work again."

I wandered out into a thick, pea-soup fog. Cars crawled along in the centre of the street; pedestrians, cloaked and muffled, hurried glumly about their business. I felt tired and ill, but it was impossible to find a taxi in weather like that, so I walked all the way home and went straight to bed.

The next day I felt, if anything, slightly worse, and as the hours crept by there was no sign of improvement. After resting for two days I returned to the Broadway Hospital. My temperature was higher than ever, and I travelled by taxi. I saw the same physician, Dr. Ground.

In the X-ray room he spent a long time examining me through the screen.

"There's a lot more fluid," he said. "We'll have to detain you as an emergency case."

My heart sank. The Broadway again. No—I could not face it. The long days of idleness, the discomfort, the boredom, the grim gaunt corridors, the bare rooms; it was like an endless prison sentence. In desperation I said:

"Must I? Couldn't I rest at home?"

"No," he said firmly. "You are very ill."

"But I must go home first to collect my things." Even an hour on parole would be better than nothing; just a taste of freedom before the gates closed on the outside world.

"I'm afraid I cannot take the responsibility of allowing you out in your condition," said Dr. Ground. "You'll have to get your things sent up."

While I was getting myself dressed again he went out to

161

arrange for a bed for me. Presently he returned, followed by a porter wheeling a chair.

"I don't need that. I can walk," I said mutinously.

"You'd better sit in it," he replied quietly.

I did so, and was taken down a long passage. At the end there was a telephone, and Dr. Ground told me I could ring up home to tell them what had happened. Then an elderly nurse came along and took my temperature. She did not smile and she did not speak to me; she behaved more like a wardress.

After about half an hour the porter came back and told me they were ready for me in a ward. The National Health Service was now in full swing, and I wondered whether the amenities were so good as the public had been told.

The ward contained ten beds; each had a wooden chair on one side and a locker on the other. There was a hush when I entered, and I was conscious of several people eyeing me curiously. A nurse came in and told me not to undress as I was to have an X-ray taken. So I was wheeled down to the familiar X-ray department, and went through the familiar Broadway Hospital procedure of queueing for a long time in a cheerless, draughty corridor. Eventually, when I returned to the ward, my hastily packed suitcase had been sent up from my home. I undressed and climbed miserably into bed. A pretty little fair-haired nurse asked me if I was all right. I told her that I was.

"You'd better have all your clothes taken away," she said. "You won't need them for a bit and there's nowhere to keep them in here."

She went on to explain that the one small cupboard in the ward had to hold all the dressing-gowns of the inmates. I asked her to pack all my belongings, and I would arrange for my suitcase to be collected the next day.

"Not to-morrow," she said. "Visiting is only allowed three times a week. An hour on Tuesday evening, an hour on Friday afternoon, and two hours on Sunday afternoon. The hospital authorities are very strict about that."

162

Dr. Ground came in to see me.

"Your trouble ought to clear up in about three weeks," he told me. "That would just let you out for Christmas. I hope you're comfortable in here."

"It's all right," I said, "but I loathe being in a ward. I hope you'll let me go home as soon as it's humanly possible."

"You'll have to be under very careful observation at present," he replied. "Of course you might like to transfer to the private wing; the rooms are smaller there and there's lots of privileges—better food and visitors every day. I'm afraid it works out at about fifteen or twenty pounds a week though."

I told him that if I was only to be in hospital for a few weeks I would prefer to stay where I was. Formerly ex-officer pensioners, when they were being treated for their pensionable disabilities, had been provided with private beds by the Ministry of Pensions, but this policy had recently been altered. I had no objection to being treated as a public patient; however, I often wondered during the succeeding days why private patients should be given quite so many advantages, and in particular why public patients should be treated so often as though they were in custody as a punishment for their past misdeeds.

Dr. Ground told me to ring my bell if I felt worse during the night, and he said he would come down to see me immediately. The man in the neighbouring bed interjected that my bell did not work.

The doctor turned to him:

"Well, you wouldn't mind ringing for him, would you?"

The man grinned. "My bell is bust too. There's only one working and it's down the far end of the ward."

"I'm sure you'll be able to attract attention somehow if anything goes wrong," said Dr. Ground.

In a short while I got to know the other patients. They were a nice lot—mainly suffering from pulmonary tuberculosis. The man in the bed opposite had been a constable in

163

the Palestine Police, and my neighbour was the barman at a West End club. The intellect of the ward was provided by a young student from the London School of Economics, and the humour—rather wearing at times—came from a small Cockney who, fortunately for me, was some way off. There was a constant din, as the head-phones behind every bed were always tuned in to the Light Programme, and it was the habit for people to plug them in and hang them on the tops of the bedsteads; I seemed to hear dance music from morning until night, from nine pairs of ear-phones, grating, muffled, and exasperating, like the brittle sound of a next-door radio.

They had all kept comparatively cheerful in spite of their long illnesses, and there was a perpetual buzz of conversation, mostly about their diseases and about women. After a few days I knew the case-history of each man in the ward, and the minute details of his sexual experiences from his early adolescence until his admission to hospital. The Sister-in-charge was extremely popular with the patients. I had met her once or twice when I had been there before. Everyone sympathised with her in having an almost hopeless task to perform, as she had under her control a complete floor, consisting of about ten wards of various sizes. To help her in this she had the services of a charge-nurse and one or two fully-trained nurses, who were as pleasant as they were efficient, but were scarcely backed up at all by a swarm of nurses under training, some of whom seemed to hate the hospital almost as much as the patients hated it. Quite a number of them should never have been in the nursing profession at all; they were callous, dirty, and idle, with no interest whatever in humanity; always watching the clock for their off-duty periods and always dodging out of the way whenever a patient rang his bell or needed attention. We had a perfect horror of a nurse she was a large, stout woman who was supposed to be looking after us in the ward. She had a rooted objection to giving any patient a blanket-bath, and indeed her one dread in life seemed to be that anyone would ask her to do anything in the way of work. The other patients told me they had grown tired of suggesting that she should bath them and the subject was now never mentioned. At first she made rather a fuss of me when she found out I was a barrister, and my second day she even volunteered to give me a bath. But when she asked me about my work and found out that I sometimes entered the Divorce Courts, she abandoned me in disgust. I discovered later that she had something of a religious mania; anyhow, from then on the only person to whom she would give any attention was my next-door neighbour, a devout Presbyterian, who worked in the West-End night-club.

I thought that the food offered to the patients was very poor indeed. One must allow, I suppose, for a certain personal fastidiousness, and also for the fact that I was feeling very sick at the time, but even to an unbiased eye the plates loaded with atrociously cooked meals of mediocre quality could hardly have been an appetising sight. And so, day after day, I watched the ward-maid tipping the scarcely-touched lunches and suppers into a portable swill-bin.

Although everyone was at pains to persuade me that my trouble was only of a very transient nature, I could not evade the presentiment that I was in for a prolonged, major illness. Each day Dr. Ground came to inspect my temperature chart, and each day he found that my fever had failed to subside. I knew my mental outlook was against me; I was unhappy, uncomfortable, and at many times almost in despair. I seemed to be totally incapable of summoning up any of that passive philosophy and stubborn determination which had helped me in my earlier illnesses. In my moments of acute depression it seemed that I had very nearly had enough.

Dr. Roberts, the specialist, came to see me; I had liked him for a long time now because I appreciated the great depths of understanding and kindliness beneath his rather detached and slightly distant professional manner. He said nothing at first, but he stood by my bedside with his hand clasping my shoulder.

Then he muttered: "I can hardly tell you how sorry I am that this should happen to you after everything else."

He told me that my trouble was partly caused by worry, which had lowered my resistance, and partly by bad luck. That I had chanced to pick up some germ or irritant which had set up inflammation and developed fluid. My artificial lung collapse would have to be abandoned forthwith.

"We will have to see how things proceed," he said, "and in the meantime I have given orders that if any crisis occurs at any time during the day or the night, I am to be summoned immediately."

He prescribed various treatments—drugs and injections. Dr. Ground had endeavoured to remove the fluid with a syringe, a process known as 'aspirating'; but, as far as I could tell, each time he managed to extract any quantity, more fluid formed in its place at once. Dr. Roberts also ordered me to take sleeping draughts as I was finding it impossible to get a good night's rest, owing to the fact that I had to sit up the whole time to counteract my breathlessness.

In the middle of December when Ground was giving me one of interminable 'aspirations' he said:

"I'm afraid you can't possibly be out for Christmas; it's going to be a longer job than we thought at first."

I found the monotony of the long, lonely days so terrible. Each time I had been in hospital before, I had had friends in to see me every afternoon, and visitors to the sick have an almost magical effect of bringing the free air of the outside world within the compass of the bedridden. They help you to escape and to forget. As it was, we all lived for the abbreviated visiting periods. The system was a strange one. All the friends and relations queued up outside the porter's lodge until the permitted time, and then they flooded into the wards. As there was only one chair for each patient, a second visitor had to sit in discomfort on the end of the bed, and a third, of course, had to stand up. When the hour was at an end a nurse walked around ringing a hand-bell, and if anyone remained for more than five minutes after that they were requested to leave immediately. Some-times, just after visiting time had commenced, a porter entered the ward with a wheel-chair to take a patient down to the X-ray department. There was no right of refusal and all protests were in vain—he would be forced to leave his friends, and if he had not returned by the end of the visiting hour, they were turned out with the rest.

It struck me then, and I have not altered my view since, that it was thoughtless and brutal for a patient undergoing a long and painful illness, from which he might never recover, to be denied the opportunity of seeing the ones he loved, for at least a short while every day.

If anyone should answer that it would be administra-tively impossible, I would point out that a number of progressive hospitals have allowed it for years past without suffering any ill effects. I can only hope that the people of this country will one day rise up in anger against any small-minded tyrants and bureaucratic die-hards who may be ruling some of their nationally-owned hospitals with a rigidity and a severity which would be more in keeping with an internment camp or a Borstal institution. Of course I realise that they have immense problems and difficulties, but the whole position should be treated in a spirit of com-promise and flexibility.

And so I spent my third Christmas in hospital, and once again I noticed that, in spite of the most strenuous efforts of the staff, something of a 'Christmas Day in the Work-house' atmosphere pervaded the ward.

One morning Sister brought in a load of decorations, and during the day the fitter patients arranged holly, ivy and mistletoe, and adorned the walls with coloured paper odd-ments. The whole thing filled me with nostalgia, so that I longed for the moment when the festivities would be at an end. I tried to forget about the house-party to which I had been invited; I tried not to think of the laughter, the freshness in young voices, the friendly crunch of footsteps in the snow, and the brightness of cheeks which had been lashed by the cold winds. Sometimes I dozed off and half-dreamt, half-thought, of the animated chatter in a crowded room, and the dancing warmth of a huge log fire. Then waking, I saw the cheap, tawdry streamers which were straggling indiscriminately throughout the ward—so brave and so pathetic.

On an evening in Christmas week the choir from a local church sang carols in the corridor, and the nurses themselves came round singing carols on Christmas Eve.

The rest of the people in the ward were rather angry when I arranged to have Communion from the hospital chaplain on Christmas morning. They did not object to the religious significance of the service, but only to the chaplain's announcement that he would be visiting me at seven o'clock. They had already been promised that the lights would not be put on until eight o'clock, so the terrible injustice of the loss of this prized and valuable extra hour of sleep caused some extremely mutinous comments. I was afraid at one time that there would be catcalls whilst Communion was being administered, but fortunately it never became as bad as that.

No temperatures or pulse readings were taken on Christmas Day, and patients were spared those distressing reminders of sickness. However, it was patently obvious to me, directly I woke up, that my temperature was still soaring.

Then there was the post. Parcels, letters, and more nostalgia. During the morning the nurses pushed the beds of the very ill patients into the lobby, and later the ambulant ones gathered round the long table which had been set out for the Christmas dinner. I lay in my bed and longed to be back in the ward. That dinner was commonly acclaimed to be the first eatable meal which any of us had tasted since our admission to the Broadway. Everyone was provided with a bottle of beer, and after votes of thanks, and a few short speeches, I was at last trundled back to the ward.

That afternoon we had a concert by the nurses followed by another from the doctors. I was told I might watch these from a wheel-chair, provided I felt up to it. The luxury of sitting out of bed was too great to be missed, and so I very untruthfully told them that I was feeling very much better. I regretted this afterwards, as I wondered several times during the performances whether I would be able to hang on until the end without fainting. At last, feeling worn out, I was returned to my bed, where I promptly fell asleep and dozed for the rest of the day.

I had hated being the focus of medical attention during my first few weeks in hospital, but I found it even more depressing after Christmas, when the novelty of my condition had ceased to interest the staff and they began to take my unremittent fever for granted. No one now spoke of my recovery or of my discharge, and in moments of blackness I wondered if I was doomed to eke out the rest of my life in those awful surroundings. The hopelessness of my struggle, the constant deterioration in my condition, and the crushing personal dejection combined to make those long-drawn days the most miserable period through which I had ever lived. Nowadays, when I try to visualise the manifold torments of hell, I recall with a shudder my timeless experiences during that winter.

Sister did a round of her patients twice a day. She was always bright and cheerful and we looked forward to seeing her. One morning she said to me:

"I've been intending to move you into a side-room, but I've not had a place until now. You'll go to-day. It's much quieter there and I think you'll prefer it."

When my colleagues heard that I was leaving they set about finding out my destination. It did not take long. The most talkative man in the ward soon dashed up to my bed to tell the results of his investigation.

"They're putting you in a double room," he said. "There's no outlook from the windows and the man you're sharing with is dying; he's been in here a year and they can't do anything for him. He's an old boy, and terribly bad-tempered."

Icy waves of despair surged over my body and my mind. Of course the move would be for the worse. Nothing good could happen ever again. When would it end? I wondered, when, oh when, would the torture cease?

CHAPTER XV

BEFORE lunch I was pushed into my new ward, a large bleak room containing two beds, one under the window and the other alongside the door. We faced out on to a courtyard which was flanked by another wing of the hospital. My neighbour, who greeted me with a nod, looked very thin, ill and shrivelled up; I could only see a shock of grey hair over a lean, gaunt face. He peered at me hard for a few moments, and then turned over and went to sleep. When lunch-time approached a sickly, greasy, cabbagey smell seeped through the open window and I noticed that a bottle of patent stench-killer had been suspended just inside. When a nurse came in, I asked her about this, and she told me that all the wards facing on to the yard found it necessary to have these bottles, because the kitchens were just underneath and the putrid stinks ascended almost the whole time. I knew that this place had won the reputation of being one of the finest Chest Hospitals in England, but, of course, it was really on account of the excellence of the doctors, the surgeons, and the general medical treatment, and most certainly not for its amenities, that it had attained this distinction.

During the afternoon Mr. Trotter, my new room-mate, spoke to me. His voice sounded weak and tired.

"I hope you won't get many visitors," he said. "I like quiet—absolute quiet. Don't talk to me—I hate chatter. I just like to sleep all day."

I told him that I understood. But I wondered how we were going to get on together. I liked people, company and conversation. Still, in spite of everything, the gloomy room, my lugubrious companion and the awful smells, I decided it was better than my last ward, with its total absence of privacy and the perpetual noise of the wireless head-phones.

That day, several nurses came to see me and remained for a few minutes asking me how I liked my new room. That was the cause of Mr. Trotter's first complaint about my behaviour: the first of a constant succession.

"I thought you understood that I wanted absolute quiet," he said angrily. "You must tell the nurses they are not to come in and gossip with you; either that, or I'll have to ask Sister to move you away again."

I felt sorry for the poor man. I heard later that he had hovered on the brink of death for almost a year, and had just turned the corner before I joined him. Now the doctors wanted him to make a strenuous effort to get back on his feet again, but he seemed to have lost the will to recover. He did not want to die, otherwise he would have slipped over the precipice long ago, but he could not find any impetus to go forward. He merely hung on where he was. He had no friends, because I do not think he had ever been a sociable or very likeable person. His only visitor was his daughter, an attractive young girl who seemed to be very devoted to him and treated him with a mixture of sternness and affection. His son, a bank clerk at Ealing, came in occasionally too, but one formed the impression that he found it a rather troublesome duty to come round and see his sick father.

Sister had told me unofficially that she did not mind my friends coming outside the proper visiting hours. She could not allow it, she said, in the large wards, but in the smaller rooms she adopted a less stringent attitude.

"I know you want cheering up," she added, "and in your case the more people you see the better."

Unfortunately illicit visits from my friends were another bone of contention between myself and Mr. Trotter. Invariably he protested directly after they had gone. It was most unfair, he used to say, for me to assume privileges just because I happened to be a barrister. The restrictions applied to me as much as to anyone else, and I should forbid my friends to visit me unless it was at the proper times.

172

Sometimes he varied his approach to the matter by passing biting criticism on my visitors, and telling me what rubbish they had talked. I never argued with him. It would be too awful, I thought, if we were quarrelling all day long, and it was far better to get myself accustomed to feeling impervious to his taunts. I do not think we ever exchanged heated words all the time we were together, but it certainly required a great deal of self-control on my side to refrain from giving a sharp answer when he was more than usually provoking.

Dr. Ground decided soon after the New Year to abandon his attempts to remove the fluids from my chest by the process of aspirating. Although this was an unpleasant enough experience, I regretted that it had proved a failure, as I did not know what alternative remedies he had in mind. It was useless to press Ground for information; he was always cagey at the best of times, and when he thought I was fishing he became an absolute oyster.

"We'll see how things go," he said; "it all depends what happens next."

Dr. Roberts was no more communicative about my future.

"We must get rid of your fever before we decide anything else."

He surveyed my chart.

"Yes, still no signs of his temperature settling down."

I was surprised when the Resident Medical Officer came round with a bundle of papers in his hand and asked me which sanatorium I should like to go to eventually.

"Need I go to any?" I asked.

"Oh, certainly. After such a severe pleural effusion you'll have to spend many months convalescing."

I told him if I must go somewhere I would like to return to Hedgely—if that could possibly be arranged. He promised to do his best, but warned me that we were now in the hands of the bureaucrats, and probably the final decision would lie with some anonymous little government clerk.

173

"When do I go?" I enquired.

He shook his head.

"I know nothing about Dr. Roberts' plans for you. You must realise you're a very sick man at the moment, and a lot depends on how your illness develops."

I started to read again, fitfully at first, and then with a certain amount of re-awakened interest. I could not get used to Mr. Trotter and his hatred of conversation. I was always forgetting. I would be glancing at the daily paper and suddenly, unthinkingly, I would remark:

"That was a fine innings of Compton's at Brisbane."

Then the instant reply, almost spat at me, from the other bed:

"I don't care a damn what Compton did at Brisbane."

I had often thought the appearance of the Broadway Hospital from the outside was as gloomy as any prison I had ever seen, yet there was a definite similarity—some people said that it looked more like a large mortuary. During those dark and dreary months after Christmas the gallery to which I belonged had an unfortunate run of deaths. The atmosphere in a ward when a patient is dying must be very like the brooding silence which hangs over a prison on the morning a condemned man is being hanged. First of all the rumour would pass round; someone would come in on his way back from the toilet:

"I hear old Jones in the big room is in a bad way. They've got him in an oxygen tent."

Sister would look drawn and worried, with the rest of the staff all showing signs of strain too. Death is not a pleasant thing even for the most hardened of us. I had often noticed during the war how the most battle-experienced troops deliberately averted their eyes when they marched past a corpse sprawled grotesquely by the roadside.

The ward-maid polishing the floor would whisper:

"Poor Mr. Jones; such a nice man. They've given up hope now; just waiting for the end, they are."

All the up-patients, with a morbid fascination, would keep us informed of his remorseless decline towards the end.

"He's rallied a bit."

"He's bad again."

"His relatives are here."

"He's unconscious."

Constant reports streamed in of the man's hopeless struggle.

The night-nurse would come round late with the evening hot drinks. We knew she had been with him, but the subject was very properly taboo as between staff and patients.

All night long a bell would ring intermittently. At the next dawn he still lived. All at once, in the middle of the morning, there would be a sudden empty silence—a tragic stillness. The nurses seemed to have vanished. Somehow, we knew what had happened even before the white-faced, dressing-gowned figure slithered round the doorway.

"Have you heard about poor old Jones? He went about an hour ago."

In time a nurse came and removed the screens from our room, placing them outside the door, which was half made of glass.

Silence again, and a trolley rumbling furtively along the passage to the mortuary. The screens taken down and replaced. The nurses affecting a forced hilarity, the sort of jollity you encounter at a funeral feast.

That evening a new patient moved into the empty bed and the routine would go on.

My barrister colleagues did their best to keep me cheerful. They paid me frequent visits and told me all about their cases, all their set-backs, and all their triumphs. Sometimes it was like one of those lunch-time conversations in Hall—only I was no longer playing any active part; they were re-living actual experiences, while I was forced back on distant, decaying memories. But I was tremendously grateful for their kindness in keeping me in touch with the

175

things which meant so much to me. I soon realised, as I learnt of their progress, that they were leaving me behind; that we were no longer stepping forward together, but they were now traversing new regions to which I had no entry. For me, it was like narrowly missing the last bus on a country lane; turning the corner, just to see it gathering way and receding in a glow of warmth and light; and standing there by the stopping place, breathless, alone, shivering, as the night blackens around and the rain patters stealthily on the bushes. Suddenly, tantalisingly, out of the distance comes the grind of changing gears, and then the silence is complete and unbroken.

Apart from friends who came to see us, the official visitors in that small, narrow world were looked forward to with great interest. Not the doctors with their guarded professional manners, nor yet the specialists with their aloof uncommunicativeness, but the volunteers who gave their ungrudging services to bring happiness to the inmates of the hospital. There were the Red Cross library ladies, who pushed round their portable bookcases once a week; somehow, out of those narrow shelves they always seemed able to find a book to suit every taste. And no trouble was too much for them; if you wanted a book especially, they invariably procured it for you. They never rushed you in your choice; they always helped you in making your selection. And, what is more, they satisfied the bed-patients' craving for ordinary conversation on subjects far removed from the hypodermic syringe and the medicine chest.

Once a week, too, the Red Cross canteen trolley visited the wards. It usually came in the evening, and the girls who brought it sometimes looked very tired. I never asked them, but I am sure they had other jobs to do during the daytime. They sold all the essential things we required in our drab, circumscribed lives. Tooth-brushes and shaving soap, writing blocks and hair lotions. But they did not wear uniform; they came from the places we had known, and they possessed a fabulous liberty—to walk out from here when their duties were finished; to go back to properly cooked meals, to their own friends and their own habits, and to sleep in the untold luxury of their own beds.

Quite by chance I discovered that Mr. Trotter had once been passionately fond of music. For an hour the barrier dropped between us, as we discussed the merits and demerits of our favourite composers and our well-loved symphonies. Then Mr. Trotter turned over and fell asleep. I do not think he ever mentioned music to me again.

January passed and February; both months were bleak and comfortless. In March the winds scurried in eddies about the yard, and mercifully the kitchen smells were largely dissipated amid gusty turbulence. I could see the wisps of cloud scudding across the small edge of sky above the red roof opposite to our window, and I thought of the countryside and the new upsurging of life which would soon transform it into an unblemished, thrilling loveliness.

At the end of March my temperature subsided and I found I could breathe with less difficulty. I had been in hospital for four months, four of the most miserable months I had ever been through.

I tackled Dr. Ground about my future.

"Will I ever be able to go back to the Bar?" I asked.

He shrugged his shoulders.

"It all depends. The fluid doesn't show any signs of disappearing yet. There is always a hope, but it would be wrong for me to pretend it was any more than a slight one at present."

When Dr. Roberts saw me a few days later he said:

"I hear you're worrying about getting back to work?"

"Yes, I find this uncertainty about the future is becoming increasingly trying."

"I know," he said. "I understand only too well. It is difficult for me to decide what to do. Normally, of course, there would be the possibility of a major operation. However, in your case—we must face it; you have been through such a lot, there is bound to be a limit to what your constitution will stand. Alternatively, I could get you up and let you go back to a very restricted life with your chest as it is."

"That means the life of a semi-invalid?" I suggested.

"That is a disagreeable term," he replied. "I'm sure you would get a lot of enjoyment out of life, even living as you would have to live."

I did not reply.

"There is another consideration too, of course," he went on. "An operation on your paralysed side might be mechanically impossible."

He went across to see Mr. Trotter. I heard him say:

"I want you to go to a sanatorium in the country. It will be a long time, a year, perhaps two years, perhaps even longer. You will gradually get up more and more until you are well enough to go home."

On his way out, Dr. Roberts stopped again by my bed.

"This business of getting back to work means a lot to you?" he said quietly.

"Yes. More than I can find words to explain."

"Then I will have a word with Mr. Barnaby Welch about your case."

Barnaby Welch was the leading chest surgeon in London. He was the man to whom my cousin had been chief assistant for several years. His name was always spoken with a shudder by patients, because it meant the ordeal of a serious chest operation, but I had met many who were walking about fit who owed their cures solely to his skill.

The idea of life as a semi-invalid filled me with horror. I thought once again of the Temple, and dreamily I pictured a Court of law. The jury has retired, the judge is out, and there is a suppressed buzz of conversation in the well of the Court and in the public gallery. Suddenly there is a flutter and flurry. The word goes round: 'Jury are coming back.' Clerks bustle away to fetch the barristers and solicitors who are smoking in the corridors and robing-rooms. The men and women of the jury file self-consciously back into their

178

seats. Warders bring up the prisoner, who tries anxiously and curiously to scrutinise the faces of his twelve fellow-citizens who have just decided his fate, but they do not return his glance; their eyes are rigidly on the ledge in front of them, or on the deserted Bench.

Silence, and the judge returns, bows, and takes his seat. Then the Clerk of the Court asks:

"Who shall speak as your foreman?"

A man in the front row rises, coughs, shuffles, and replies: "I will."

"Have you agreed on your verdict?" asks the clerk. Involuntarily everyone in that court-room leans forward slightly.

"We have."

"Do you find the accused man guilty or not guilty?"

In tense stillness the clock above the judge ticks loudly, ponderously, methodically.

Could it be true that I would have to say good-bye to all that? That I would never again sit in wig and gown as one of the principals, one of the contestants, in that fascinating human arena?

After that, events took shape fairly rapidly.

One evening a couple of nurses rushed in and began to straighten my bedclothes.

"Mr. Welch is doing an unexpected round," they told me, "and he's coming to see you."

I could not suppress a feeling of strained anxiety. So much depended on the few words the surgeon would say to me. Mr. Trotter was reading a book, apparently uninterested.

Voices outside, and the door was thrown open.

Barnaby Welch, a small, neat, smiling figure, came in and walked to the side of my bed followed by four doctors; his secretary, the Sister, and a nurse, all grouped round him.

He shook hands with me.

"Yes, I remember you at your cousin's wedding," he said, and then without wasting any time he went on: "I've

179

looked at your X-rays just now. You're in a mess and something's got to be done about it. If you leave here with your chest as it is now, you'll live with a sword of Damocles constantly suspended over your head. This is bound to catch up on you eventually, and I think it would be sooner rather than later."

"What would you suggest, sir?" I asked.

I was annoyed to hear my voice sounding rather hoarse, like the voices of prisoners, just convicted, when they are asked if they have anything to say before sentence is passed on them according to the law. I felt, in many ways, as a man must feel standing in the dock at such moments, waiting patiently for the judge to pronounce his punishment.

"I want you to allow me to operate on you. Give me *carte blanche* to open up your chest and to do whatever I find necessary. But once we have put our hands to the plough there can be no turning back. I will try to remove a portion of your right lung. However, I cannot say at the moment; I may find it necessary to take away the whole lung, but I assure you I will leave as much of it as I possibly can."

"All right, sir," I said again in a hoarse croak. "I'll agree."

"Well done, old chap. Well done," he murmured. He turned sharply and walked out followed by his retinue, none of whom looked back.

The door closed behind them and the room was absolutely still. After a few minutes Mr. Trotter said:

"If they operate soon, you'll be taken away from here."

I detected a note of hopefulness in his voice.

"I suppose so," I said. "I'm afraid you haven't been very happy with me as your companion."

He was lying on his back, motionless, looking at the ceiling.

"No," he said, "I haven't. It's not anything you've done, it's your character. I've heartily disliked you from the start."

180

"Why?" I asked. Anything to take my mind off what Mr. Welch had just told me.

"I've been a chartered accountant all my life," said Mr. Trotter, "and I like people and things which fit into a pattern. But you—you're so flamboyant. I hate a personality like yours; I always have done; you're too exuberant. The nurses have told me I'm jealous of you, but they're wrong; it's simply that I detest you more and more every day, and I can't help myself."

"Well," I replied, "it won't be much longer now. Barnaby Welch operates once a week down at Hedgely, and I'm going to try to arrange for him to deal with me down there."

Dr. Ground came to see me that evening. I asked him what my prospects were after the operation.

"It's difficult to say," he informed me. "It is a big operation—a very big one. You ought to know that before you decide anything. Even if it's successful, it's problematical how much you will be able to do in the future."

I pressed him for a direct answer, and eventually he said:

"This is only a presumption, but I should think that if you lost the whole lung, you would probably be unable to practise as a barrister: if you were to lose only a part, you might be able to go back."

Before he went away he added:

"The brighter side of the picture is worth thinking about too. If the operation is a success, and you stand up to it, you will be completely rid of your chest trouble."

The prospect of a major operation in the near future came as a great shock to me at first, but gradually I grew accustomed to the idea, and my mind became readjusted to the situation.

At any rate this was a tangible danger; a brisk, mortal peril, which sweeps by you in a mad moment of intense fear; like the overhead scream of a shell or the whine of a sniper's bullet. It is there and then it is gone. Either you fall or you continue, crouching and stumbling on your way.

181

CHAPTER XVI

THE authorities acceded to my request for a transfer to Hedgely. Dr. Roberts wrote to Dr. Pearce and explained the situation, and the latter replied that he would find me a vacancy at his sanatorium within the next fortnight. Sister gave me this news and then added with a smile:

"So we'll soon be able to go back to our proper visiting times."

"I haven't had many illicit visitors lately, Sister," I protested.

"Well, you've got one now, waiting outside. Rather a nice blonde. I'll tell her she can come in."

I heard an angry snort from Mr. Trotter.

"It won't be long now," I said.

"Thank God for that," he added shortly.

For half an hour Hazel and I chatted pleasantly. Then she said:

"By the way, I've been speaking about you to an aunt of mine. She was very interested. She'd like to come and see you if you wouldn't mind."

I said: "Of course not."

"She might be able to help you. She's just taken up some healing business. Apparently she's got a special gift; she just waves her hands about and people are cured."

I sighed. People had tried to put me on to quack remedies so often before.

"Does she conjure up goblins?" I asked, "so that they can dance round the patient's bed until he recovers?"

"Don't be frivolous," she reproved. "As a matter of fact, the scheme is run by the Church. And it isn't a racket either; it is an entirely voluntary effort and there's no charge at all."

"By all means let your aunt come if she wants to," I told

Hazel. "I make no promises, but I'm always willing to hear from anyone who has ideas on how I could get better."

A few days later a Mrs. Winteringham came to see me. She was a lady with a pleasing personality, and I took to her immediately. Her manner was bright and humorous, understanding and kind, sincere and generous. Although she was aflame with a restless energy, yet there were times when she wore the mystical vagueness of the unrepentant visionary.

I wondered when she was going to mention the purpose of her visit, as she left the subject of my illness and started to talk about general matters. Then, following a pause in the conversation, she looked at me hard and smiled.

"So you think I'm practising a form of black magic?"

"No, not really," I laughed too. "But there are so many well-meaning eccentrics about, to say nothing of the charlatans who make a comfortable living off the hopeless and unfulfilled dreams of the sick."

"I can't think what Hazel must have told you about my work, in her airy-fairy way—bless her! She's really quite keen now, and she's going to help us out from time to time with her car."

"I haven't got the foggiest notion what you really do," I said.

"Well, I'd better tell you. Doubtless you'll want to cross-examine me pretty thoroughly when I'm finished, but that's only as it should be."

I waited while Mrs. Winteringham went on:

"We call ourselves 'The Churches' Council of Healing'. The council was created by Archbishop Temple towards the end of the recent war. He had always believed that healing was a threefold business; you had to treat the body, the mind, and the spirit. We offer no substitute for the doctor and the surgeon, but we seek to co-operate with them, and to approach healing from an additional angle."

"I don't know that doctors would entirely approve," I said.

"On the contrary, the British Medical Association is entering whole-heartedly into the work and they have nominated their own representatives to sit on the Council."

"What do you suggest for me?" I enquired.

"Merely that, if you are willing, I intend to put your name before a prayer group, who will pray for the successful outcome of the treatment your medical advisers prescribe."

"And what do I have to do?"

"Nothing much. Of course it would help if you could make yourself really believe. Before you go to sleep every night, simply tell God that you trust in Him and ask Him to let the best happen."

"The best?"

"Yes. Don't tell Him what to do. Let things work out according to His Will."

"And supposing the operation does not come off? Supposing I die?"

"Well; do you fear death so very much?" she enquired.

"I don't know. Sometimes, when I am in pain, the prospect of death seems sweet and merciful—like the shade of a great tree when you've been walking for a long time in the sweltering heat of a fierce sun. And then the pain eases, and I want nothing more than to cling on desperately to life, despite all its torments."

"If His plan for you is death, then He will help you to view it without dread."

"I think I fear even more the thought that I will drag on for years and years without ever again leaving my bed."

"If that is what He has decided for you, then again, He will help you to go through with it. You see, that is why you do not pray for recovery. That would be too easy. But in reality you will be praying for His assistance in whatever may lie ahead."

The light was fading and the smell of frying potatoes flooded the room.

Mr. Trotter coughed uneasily.

"D'you mind if I put on my light?"

"Not at all," said Mrs. Winteringham.

He pulled himself up on his pillows and fiddled with the switch above his head. Presently a pale circle of light played on the top of his bed. He glared at Mrs. Winteringham with obvious distaste and then settled down to his book. She smiled, but did not seem to mind. She turned to me again:

"Of course, you will hope. We will all hope. What would suit you best?"

"I don't really want an operation," I said, "on account of the discomfort and the risk. On the other hand, if I were to have one, and they could remove only the bad part of my lung, I suppose it would be perfect for me."

"Well, carry on hoping. You know, much illness has its origin in spiritual uncertainty—a sort of all-embracing disharmony. The power of God can help and heal."

She was silent.

"Why is it called the 'Churches' Council'?" I asked.

"Because all sorts of Churches are represented on it, such as the Baptists, the Methodists, and the Society of Friends, and many more."

"I'd like you to put down my name," I told her. "I believe it will help me."

She stood up.

"Good!" she said. "Well, I must go and visit some more people. I will look you up again at the sanatorium, and you must keep in touch with me and tell me how you get on."

CHAPTER XVII

In the back of my mind I felt that everything was going to be all right, but I was by no means certain. It seemed to be such a natural termination to my life; an unsuccessful operation; a sporting chance which did not come off. I had a longing to see my home once again; just for a brief few hours; to rest in my own room, surrounded by my books; to sleep in my own bed; to look out of the window in the early morning on the familiar scene which had met my waking glance so often before.

I spoke about this to Sister.

"What exactly do you want?" she asked.

"I'd like to go home before I go down to Hedgely; not for long. Just for a day and a night."

"But why?"

"Well—just in case."

"Oh," she said, "I see. Yes, I'll certainly try to arrange it, but don't tell Dr. Roberts your reason; I don't think he'd like it."

As I was weak from the months I had spent in bed, I was told I could start getting up several times a day, just to walk along to the toilet. I was not to do anything more than stroll slowly to and fro. It was a compromise between causing a relapse through overstrain and climbing on to the operating table with no strength at all in my limbs.

At last the moment arrived. Sister came in the door holding a letter in her hand.

"They want you down at Hedgely after lunch next Friday."

We discussed how I should get there, and she suggested that I could go home the previous day in a taxi and she would arrange for an ambulance to pick me up there and drive me down to the sanatorium. But later on she told me that the National Health authorities would not grant a permit for an ambulance to drive more than a certain distance unless the patient was so ill that he could not possibly walk at all. In my case, I did not come within the necessary category, so I would be driven by ambulance to Waterloo Station and I would travel to Hedgely by train, with an ambulance meeting me at the station there. She agreed that it would be rather an ordeal after five months in bed to get up, dress, and find my way round a busy London terminus.

"I'm afraid we are just a branch of the Civil Service now," she sighed. "We no longer have any discretion like we used to have; it's all forms and documents these days."

As a matter of fact, an old friend of mine came in shortly afterwards and I told him the story. He would not hear of my attempting a train journey, and offered to drive me down to Hedgely in his car. It was all arranged, and Dr. Roberts gave his approval and also granted me permission to go home the day before my admission to the sanatorium.

Things were beginning to move. I felt as though, after being stranded for a long while in the stagnant waters of a side-stream, I was now once again caught up in the fresh surge and flow of the main channel.

On the morning of my departure from the Broadway Hospital, I put on my clothes for the first time since that agonising day before Christmas. I said good-bye to the staff and to my fellow-patients; it was difficult to know who felt more jubilant on this occasion—Mr. Trotter or myself. Then my sister arrived in a taxi, and I went home and straight to bed.

That brief interlude at home resembled one of those snatched war-time leaves when everything used to be so fleeting and hectic, and the ephemeral minutes passed, with every tick of the clock making an appreciable inroad, as certain and as relentless as the encroachment of a rising tide.

A lot of friends came in in the afternoon, and I put on a

187

dressing-gown and had tea with them in the sitting-room. I had told very few people about my operation; we all agreed that it would be advisable not to inform my mother until the very last moment before it took place, to save her a long period of worry. Of course there was nothing definitely arranged. Dr. Roberts was still hoping an alternative solution would present itself, and Mr. Barnaby Welch had made the reservation that he would have to decide at the appropriate moment if an operation was a justifiable proposition. So nobody mentioned surgery on that afternoon, but I noticed that, when each one was leaving and he shook me by the hand and bade me 'Good luck', there was something in his strength of grasp and in the sincerity of his voice which made it clear that their feelings and their sympathy would be with me when the time came.

In the evening we had a family dinner-party in my bedroom. It was high-spirited and most enjoyable.

Before I went to sleep that night I prayed: "O God, may the best happen." It was hard not to add: "Please do not take all this away from me."

The following day was crisp and blue, and we drove down to Hedgely in the tepid sunlight of early spring.

The familiar drive, the familiar entrance hall, induced a wave of revulsion in my mind. This was a place to which I had said good-bye and to which I had never intended to return. And yet a friendly, peaceful atmosphere still dominated the great building, as it had done on my first visit. A porter had come to my room carrying my suitcase for me. In the passage we met a pretty, auburn-haired nurse.

"Why, Mr. Tobias," she greeted me. "We expected you to arrive on a stretcher."

"I can walk all right," I said, but in truth my legs felt as though they had had about enough.

"Well, would you get into bed, please, and I'll bring you some tea."

She opened the door of a large room.

188

"Here you are. I hope you'll be comfortable."

I walked in. Everything was spotlessly clean and was freshly painted. The glass doors leading on to the balcony were wide open, and there, once again, I saw the magnolia trees in full blossom, the wistaria-covered alcoves, and in the distance the gentle gracefulness of the rolling South Downs. I went over to the window and looked out across the gardens. Then I thought of my barren ward at the Broadway, the yard outside and all its smells. I was suddenly filled with a conviction which I had also experienced on the day of my previous arrival, that I must get better here; misfortune was impossible amid all this tranquillity and loveliness.

When I was in bed a doctor visited me to take down my case history. He was a tall, athletically-built Australian of about thirty who had a manner which at once inspired confidence. He told me his name was Dr. Grant. I was hoping I would be allowed to get up for at least one meal a day, but he informed me it was too great a risk to take. Instead he gave me permission to walk to the toilet as often as I chose, and to have a proper bath twice a week.

"I suppose you want to get the operation behind you," he said, "and I'll do what I can to get your name high up on Mr. Welch's waiting list."

During the evening various patients from the near-by rooms came in to introduce themselves. This floor had always had the name of being the most friendly in the sanatorium; certainly I was very impressed by the kindness of all my neighbours. The moving spirit among them was the present Chairman of the Patients' Committee, an Air Vice-Marshal who had recently been knighted. Always known as 'The A.V.M.', he was immensely popular and greatly respected. He had a deep sense of duty and tried to visit all his bed-patient friends at least once a day. Whenever he came into my room and the other people there stood up out of courtesy, he always became greatly embarrassed.

"You know—really. This is quite unnecessary," he would say. "I'm retired now and frightfully unimportant."

This modest behaviour only served to increase the esteem in which he was held by all of us.

The A.V.M. was about the last person to feel sorry for himself. He knew he was very ill and that at best the doctors would only be able to patch him up. Only once did he reveal his true feelings to me. On that occasion he was alone in my room, watching a game of clock-golf going on outside. Suddenly he said:

"Do you play golf, Toby?"

"No," I replied. "I intended to take it up when I was too old for rugger, but I've never got down to it."

"I was always very fond of the game myself," he said. "I planned to play a great deal when I retired."

He came over and sat down in the basket-chair.

"It's funny how you spend so much time looking forward to your retirement, and thinking you'll do all sorts of things which you've always wanted to do but never had the time—and then something happens like this, and all your day-dreams come back to taunt you with their hollow mockeries."

He glanced at me and became embarrassed.

"Of course I shouldn't talk like that, really."

He started to speak of other things. I knew he was annoyed with himself for allowing me to see behind the curtain for even a brief moment.

Our Floor Representative was a middle-aged man who spent all his time painting. He had had a full and interesting life in which he had been at various times a soldier, a barrister, a successful playwright, and a Secret Service agent. He was married to a very well-known actress, and he was obviously very fond of her and very proud. Everyone called him 'Flakers', and his sense of humour, puckish, sparkling, and effervescent, enlivened the atmosphere of the whole floor.

Next door to me was David, a barrister in the Army

190

Legal Service. He was just starting to get up and spent most of the day sitting in my room.

We had also a quota of Naval, Army, and Royal Air Force officers, mostly down the far end of the corridor. Sandwiched among them was the managing director of a prosperous family cotton business in Egypt. The 'Pasha', as we called him, was a very intelligent man and most amusing; he was, however, a perpetual *poseur* and would become rather irritating at times. Admittedly he was a fluent, forceful, and witty speaker, but whenever he was about, the discussion quickly turned into a monologue. Even the long-suffering A.V.M. said to me once:

"The first thing I do whenever the Pasha comes into a room is to get up and leave it."

When I had been at Hedgely for a few weeks I had settled down perfectly and grown very attached to the other men on my floor. All except me were in the process of finishing off their treatment and, as a result, since I had my operation to come, they used to treat me with especial kindness.

It became the accepted practice for anybody who was at a loose end in the evening to bring his going-to-bed drink into my room, and it was customary for me to have at least half a dozen visitors there, all joining in an animated and cheerful conversation. One could not be depressed in such company and, what was more, there were several people with tastes and interests similar to my own. David was devoted to music; the Pasha had studied philosophy; Flakers loved to reminisce about his briefless days at the Bar before he had launched his first successful play in the West End. And, of course, the A.V.M., humorous and unassuming, whose opinions on all subjects were so clear-sighted and so eminently sensible.

Later on a newcomer moved into the room on one side of mine. He was a schoolmaster, and he also was awaiting a transfer over to the surgical wing. We became very friendly and he used to talk to me about his religious convictions, for he was a devoted member of the Society of

191

Friends. During the war he had registered as a conscientious objector and he was put to work as a farm labourer. He was still an ardent pacifist, which led to a great deal of amiable argument with the rest of us. Like the majority of Quakers he was utterly sincere, and I found his simple kindliness a very endearing quality.

I was able to do a good deal of reading, as it was considered essential for me to obtain the maximum amount of rest. I divided up my day into set periods of history, philosophy, and novel reading, with the idea of keeping my brain alert and attentive. Inevitably, I had plenty of time to think, and I was surprised to find that I could face the future without any considerable fear. I decided that this was due to some psychological device, some mental trick which was suppressing my real feelings. The day will come, I thought, when I shall feel a natural terror. Yet I was thankful that that day had not yet arrived. The idea that some members of the Churches' Council of Healing were thinking of me and praying for my recovery was very comforting, and helped me to achieve a considerable mental peacefulness and a passive serenity. The only real happiness in this world is possessed by those who, irrespective of surrounding circumstances, have minds which are calm and untroubled. I found that the rapidly approaching crisis in my life added a great depth to my feelings. I recalled a description in Dostoevsky's *The Idiot*, telling of a man in France on his way to the guillotine. He knew that this was to be his last journey, but he was not thinking of the blade and the executioner; instead his eyes were feasting avidly on the scenes in the streets through which he passed, and he saw more clearly and experienced more acutely than ever before, because his end was so near. Dostoevsky must surely have drawn on his personal knowledge, as he himself had been sentenced to death, led to the gallows, and reprieved at the eleventh hour. Of course, I did not feel melancholy about the outcome of my operation; it was simply that I had to face the definite possibility of death, and that fact seemed to add a new significance to all that was happening around me; it lent me, too, a far deeper perception during the period which separated me from that final moment on the operating table, when I would close my eyes and enter into the labyrinths of that hazardous sleep.

The weather was beautiful and every morning, before breakfast, we would all stroll on the balcony to watch the rising sun light up the hills with its dancing, quivering shafts. The Pasha was in his element in moments such as these. Standing there silently, a pipe in his mouth, black beard flowing over a crimson dressing-gown, for twenty minutes he would not twitch a muscle. I could not help wondering if this strange behaviour was not inspired by stories of the impassive meditations of Socrates on the prayer ground.

The doctors left me alone. There was nothing to be done until Mr. Welch gave the word.

About this time I received a curious communication from the grey squirrel who used to visit the rooms every day for tit-bits of food. The object of the letter was, apparently, to complain about the quality of some cake which I had given him the previous day. That was the first of a series of notes which I would find in my room when I returned from shaving in the morning. They were always couched in a witty and humorous style, strangely similar to that in which Flakers was accustomed to write his farces. They caused me and my colleagues a great deal of amusement, but Flakers himself would never admit to their authorship.

The staff on that floor were a delightful lot. The Sister-in-charge was an intelligent woman, who kept very much to herself, but managed all our daily lives with great efficiency. The pretty, auburn-haired staff nurse was the second-in-command. She was very popular with the patients, and always doing whatever she could to help them. We had one other nurse, a fat, laughing, lovable woman from Sweden, who had come to this country to learn the language, and so far had made very little progress. Finally there were two attractive German ward-maids, who were always cheerful and obliging.

On one occasion there was a temporary rift in the lute. The younger of the German girls was away on leave and her place was taken by a very temperamental Central European. She was quite unable to cope with the recognised system by which patients who had completed their morning ablutions, and had had their beds made up, gave four rings on the bell to signify they were ready for breakfast.

Her method was to work her way along the passage, placing the trays in each room in turn, whether the occupant was present or not. After I had endured a cold breakfast for three mornings I told her it was not good enough.

"It is my way," she replied testily. "You get used to it. How do you say? You like it or you lump it."

After this inconclusive discussion I made up my mind that I most certainly did not like it, and I would be very loath to lump it, as she had suggested.

The following morning the ward-maid saw me down the length of the corridor, just entering a bathroom to shave.

"Mr. Tobias," she called, "your breakfast in."

I shouted back that I would not be ready for at least ten minutes. When I returned to my room the tray had been taken away again. I gave the requisite four rings, but I discovered that my bell had been disconnected. Eventually I found out that she had disconnected all the bells. I discovered her in the kitchen.

"Ah," she muttered. "You play me up—I play you up. You get no breakfast. Several others get no breakfast this morning as punishment. You all learn to do things my way."

I located the Sister and told her the whole story. The result was that I had my breakfast, and the turbulent Austrian was transferred to housemaid's work in the Sisters' Home.

No Memorial

It is strange how one can shut one's mind completely to something unpleasant which must come at last, swiftly and inevitably. 'And when the angel with his darker draught draws up,' one is totally unprepared to take it without shrinking. Of course I knew that the moment was drawing near, but the atmosphere was so deceptively silent—like that tense, unearthly stillness which suddenly settled over front-line trenches before a violent battle. When the door opened and Mr. Welch walked in with Dr. Pearce, I stared at them scarcely believing. I could hear my heart thumping wildly. Mr. Welch came straight across the room and sat on the side of my bed, while Dr. Pearce stood with his back towards me, looking out of the window.

"Well, old chap," said Mr. Welch quietly, "the time has come. I'm willing if you are. Let's get this quite clear. You must give me *carte blanche*—nothing less. Once I start there's no turning back. Dr. Roberts fully agrees with me. You know all the risks; you've been a soldier and faced dangers before. Now—what do you say?"

"I'm willing to go ahead," I replied.

"Capital, old chap, capital!" He reached forward and squeezed my shoulder. "There's something more you should know. If I have to remove the whole lung, you'll have to undergo another major operation four weeks later; even if I only remove a part, it may still be necessary. In view of your other wounds and disabilities, this second operation may cause a bit of disfigurement."

"I can only hope," I said, struggling hard to prevent my voice reflecting the dread that surged up in my heart at his words.

Then Dr. Pearce spoke.

"I'll merely say that I think Mr. Welch is taking the only course that will give you any chance in the future. I know it's not a pleasant one, but we sometimes have to take these great risks when we are faced with a condition that is hopelessly incurable without pretty drastic surgical treatment."

They both went to the door. As they were going out Mr. Welch turned and said:

"Bad luck isn't rationed in this life, Tobias; if it was, you would probably have nothing more to worry about for a long time to come."

I think the word went round the floor very quickly, because the others scarcely left me alone for five minutes for the next few days.

First of all came Flakers to tell me what had happened to him that morning. Apparently during the rest-hour he had noticed something irritating in his eye. When the final bell sounded he had rushed along to the kitchen to borrow an eye-bath in order to wash out the foreign body. There were three people in the kitchen, the Swedish nurse and the two German maids, and Flakers found that it was beyond all his ingenuity to explain what he wanted. For five minutes he gave a lively miming display, imitating a man douching out his eyes with an eye-bath. The three stood round him with puzzled frowns on their faces. Suddenly the Swede gave an exclamation. She smiled broadly and let Flakers down to a young sub-lieutenant's room. She went up to his bedside cupboard, threw it open, and proudly revealed a half-full bottle of rum. Flakers hastened to tell her that what he wanted was not a prohibited alcoholic drink, but a perfectly legitimate medical appliance.

While I was laughing at the story he suddenly became serious:

"So your moment has arrived. I do hope it will be a tremendous success. I've just got my date. I'm leaving in exactly a week. We must meet in London later on."

The A.V.M. told me that he too had received his marching orders.

"It will be nice to get home again," he said pensively. "But it's a pretty curtailed existence. Breakfast in bed every morning, and I'm not allowed to stay up after eight o'clock at night. I told them I'd prefer an operation.

Apparently there's not much hope of that, because the disease has too much hold in both my lungs. I'm sorry I won't be here, Toby, while you have your little effort, but I'll keep in touch and look you up when I return for an overhaul next month."

The Sister told me that David seemed far more worried than I was myself.

"If we don't operate on you soon to put him out of his misery, he'll be having a relapse," she laughed.

The day after Mr. Welch's visit Mrs. Winteringham turned up unexpectedly at tea-time.

"I climbed into my car after lunch," she said. "I didn't know where I was going—I just drove on. Then I saw a sign-post which said 'Hedgely', so I knew my destination at once."

I told her my news and she was delighted.

"Of course I had hoped that you wouldn't have to have this operation, but I don't think you'll regret it. It's bound to be for the best."

Mrs. Winteringham worked under a ministrant who had been the fount and impetus of the Church Healing Movement since its foundation. He was old now, and for years he had been absolutely blind, but he still devoted all his time, his talents, and his energies to the work of healing. People who had come into contact with him were lost in wonder and admiration at his goodness and his tremendous love for his fellow-men. He had, too, an unexplained power, as though a great and mysterious force was working through him for the good of mankind. There was something angelic, and something miraculous, about this man and the way he journeyed hither and thither going wherever he felt he was needed; helping, healing, aiding and comforting the sick and the oppressed.

"If you want to see him before your operation, he'll come to you," said Mrs. Winteringham. "But I don't think it's necessary."

"Neither do I," I replied, thinking of all the manifold

calls on the ministrant's time. People in far worse plights than my own needed him more.

"I was speaking to him about you last week, and he thinks it will be all right."

She told me to let her know the exact time of my operation, so that the group who were responsible for my welfare could make their arrangements.

As Mrs. Winteringham sat there chatting amiably with me, I reflected how she radiated spiritual strength. She was obviously possessed of absolute faith; not an arrant belief in her own safety, but an implicit trust which would enable her to meet all the brutalities of existence, and yet to be inspired—even unto the end—by the selfless love of a Master to whom she had given such devoted service.

She went away, walking jauntily and briskly down the passage. She was obviously very pleased, but she seemed as detached and unconcerned as though she had been viewing with approval some friend's carefully cultivated herbaceous border.

CHAPTER XVIII.

THERE were two chaplains at Hedgely, and the contrast
between their personalities was as interesting as it was
pleasing. They came to the sanatorium in turn from a
neighbouring village.

The elder of the two was a middle-aged man. He had
been a naval padre and, in his youth, a great oarsman. The
first time I met him I formed an immediate impression of
unbounded kindliness and infinite understanding. Christianity for him was not a negative or a prohibitive creed;
its teaching was not confined to a destructive, puritanical
'Thou shalt not'. As he envisaged the teaching of Jesus
Christ, it was something creative, all-absorbing, and essentially joyful. The Christian was not obliged to walk, glum-
faced, down a narrow lane through the mass of unbelievers;
he was not forced to stand apart from the crowd, solitary
and self-righteous; rather he should move among them and
be one of themselves. But his light would always be fuller;
his purpose more steadfast; his heart more contented; his
faith less vulnerable. Until, at last, the atheist would
admire and envy, and even come to share his beliefs.

This chaplain did not visit the patients to spout religion
at them. When he came to see me we used to talk about
many things, and our conversation would range pleasurably
from the music of Sibelius to the chaplain's latest litter of
cocker spaniel puppies.

The curate was about my own age. He had entered Holy
Orders rather late in his life and had formerly been an
engineer; in fact, he had served as a Sapper officer during
the war and had lost a leg in Holland. He too was kind and
charming, but some of the patients found his philosophy
was a little intense. He certainly had all that devout

sincerity of the convert or, at any rate, of one who surges forward in the tumultuous energy of a reawakened belief.

These two, the vicar and the curate, impressed me as being amongst the finest clergymen I had ever met. Both were absolutely devout, generous, loving, considerate, broad-minded, and sincere. They worked well together; the younger providing a continual impetus—the constant stimulus of a restless energy—and the elder stemming the eager flow with tact and kindliness; bringing to bear his maturer wisdom, his greater worldly knowledge and judgment.

I felt that both of them regarded God as a loving and devoted Father; though, perhaps, in the curate's conception He was slightly more aloof, but, at the same time, just and forgiving and understanding.

Every Thursday morning one of the chaplains would visit each bed-patient who had asked for Holy Communion, and afterwards he would take a service in the small lounge for anyone who was clothed, or who was permitted to wander about in a dressing-gown. On Sunday nights they officiated at Evensong.

Communion can mean a lot to the sick; there is something immensely moving and personal about the whole service. It is easy enough to attend Morning Prayer, and to follow the familiar routine in the set sequences of a drill parade. It is so simple to pray half-heartedly and inattentively like Christopher Robin:

> "God bless Mummy. I know that's right.
> Wasn't it fun in the bath to-night?"

But Communion is essentially individual and private, and it is difficult not to feel deeply and to experience something tantamount to a spiritual shower-bath when one partakes in it.

You cannot but be struck by the beautiful language of

the prayers; by their simplicity and fullness of meaning. Take this, for instance:

"We do not presume to come to this Thy Table, O merciful Lord, trusting in our own righteousness, but in Thy manifold and great mercies."

And the Blessing at the conclusion of the service must be one of the most wonderful, most comforting, and most heartening sentences which has ever been written in our language:

"The peace of God, which passeth all understanding, keep your hearts and minds in the knowledge and love of God, and of His Son, Jesus Christ, our Lord; and the blessing of God Almighty, the Father, the Son, and the Holy Ghost, be amongst you and remain with you always."

I often thought it was a great pity that so few patients at the sanatorium availed themselves of this eternal consolation. I occasionally spoke about it to my closer friends. They would shrug their shoulders:

"It's all very well," they would say, "I suppose I'm a Christian, but I'm not a churchgoer. If you can get something out of it, all I can say is that you're very lucky."

I would tell them that I was not by any means a deeply religious man. Neither would I ever attempt to become an evangelist. In every faith there must be a few leaders, and there must also be a host of followers. The best and the purest must lead, and the lesser and the weaker must follow.

Every realist will admit that if Christian doctrines could spread into, and could eventually dominate, every branch of our lives, it would go a long way towards solving a great many of the problems of our present-day existence.

The fundamental of the Christian faith is Love. Who will dispute that the greater part of the unpleasantness of the world is caused by envy, malice, and hatred? If only twenty million people in this country commenced each day by really forgiving all others their trespasses against them, clearing their hearts and their minds of every bitterness and antagonism, what a magical effect it would have on the community generally!

I always avoided a religious argument because of my lack of skill and my lack of knowledge. Also, because I hesitated to propound any principles of Christian ethics whilst being only too well aware of the constant lapses and frailties of my own life. I fancied that my silence was more beneficial than my propaganda would ever have been. A true faith thrives on tolerance just as it withers with pedantry.

When I was very young, I was sent to a small preparatory school owned and run by a strict and narrow-minded Scottish headmaster. All the boys used to live through the whole week dreading the torments of the following Sunday, because the whole of the Sabbath was devoted to silence, church-going, and compulsory Bible reading. Even now, when I look back through the vista of the years, I can feel again the grim horror of the protracted hours during which we were compelled to sit silently at our desks with the open pages of the Old Testament in front of us and the eagle eye of the headmaster ever watchful for symptoms of wandering attention.

Worse still, all pastimes were forbidden on Sunday except meek conversation and long, organised, country walks in crocodile. If any boy was caught wrestling, ragging, or playing any game, he received a severe caning first thing on Monday morning. Such an environment must have formed a ready breeding ground for paganism.

Others who unconsciously harm the Church are those who parade their worship every Sunday morning, and who openly despise anybody who does not choose to occupy a place in the pew which forms the only acceptable mark of gentility and of God-fearing respectability. Often these people are well known to be narrow and mean in their private lives, and the young and the sensitive almost involuntarily shun their company.

Sometimes I am asked how I can possibly go on believing in a God of Love after all I have suffered. That is a very searching question to which I feel I ought to make some reply. The truth of the matter is that I have no real regrets for what I have been through. I could not possibly deny the agony of mind which I endured when I first became aware that my incapacities were permanent and that my right arm would be virtually useless for as long as I lived. I cannot deny that moments of bitterness and black despair occasionally haunt me even now in the chill, quiet hours of the night. But the fact remains that I have been taught to do without my useless limb. I have gradually been given physical independence and mental peace regarding my disability. I cannot even begin to explain why an omnipotent God allows so much suffering throughout all His creation. William Temple once said: "A world in which both suffering and sympathy exist is preferable to one with neither." I admit that that provides a meagre consolation. I suppose you can only fall back on the old tag that a great many things are beyond human understanding. And perhaps I might add, with the experience of one who has known a certain degree of pain and a certain degree of misfortune, that nothing turns out to be nearly so bad when it actually happens to you personally; you quickly grow accustomed to your loss, in such a way that the joyfulness of life is in no way dimmed.

If it be a valid argument for the non-existence of God that the world is full of evil, pain and ugliness, it must surely be legitimate to reply that Christ is also responsible for all the beautiful things. Whenever I hear Beethoven's 'Pastoral Symphony'; whenever I look at a sculpture of Michelangelo's or a painting by Leonardo da Vinci; or whenever I see a flash of white skirts as the *corps de ballet* swing into one of those sadly-gay waltzes in Chopin's *Les Sylphides*— then I invariably think of the hand of God. It is always around us; the smile of excitement that lights up a young face will surely outweigh a thousand and one tears of sorrow. The greatest sadness is that the world does not see it. It was written centuries ago:

"He was in the world, and the world was made by him, and the world knew him not."

That is still the tragedy of to-day.

· · · · ·

When the date of my operation was finally settled, I was told I might get up and dress for tea every day during the interim period. I had been in bed for almost eight months and it was considered advisable that I should gather up a little strength before undergoing surgery. It made a pleasant break going along to the dining-hall, and my friends spoiled me to an absurd extent, refusing even to let me refill my own tea-cup.

One afternoon the Sister informed me that I was moving immediately to the operating wing. The staff nurse packed up my possessions and accompanied me, carrying my suitcase. My new room was very small, but comfortable enough. The windows faced out on to the front drive and the gently sloping forest path known as the Pine Walk. The operating wing had only recently been opened and it was ultra-modern and, for a hospital, exceedingly luxurious, every room containing a built-in wardrobe, a basin with running hot water, and an arm-chair.

I was expecting the realisation of what was in store to strike suddenly and to fill me with apprehension, but I still found that my mind continued calm and peaceful. And yet, I thought, the fear and dread must come; the calm and the peacefulness would be ripped away in a moment, to reveal the stark truth of what lay ahead.

Both chaplains came to me to wish me luck. The elder stayed in my room for half an hour. Before he left, he looked out of the window at some of the medical orderlies who were playing an improvised cricket match on the lawn.

I could not see them, but I could hear the swiftly-running footsteps, the eager cries, and the sharp reports as the leather ball was struck by the batsman.

He turned round.

"Well, how do you feel?"

"Not so bad as I had feared."

"It's rather like the moment before a race," he said reminiscently. "How the seconds drag when you're waiting for your starting orders!" I knew his mind had receded into the past, re-living his hours of carefree glory on the river. And I thought back, too, of the moments, sitting erect in the boat, blades resting on the surface, and the steady chug-chug-chug of the umpire's launch as it turned and edged slowly into position between the rival boats.

"I must go now," he said. "You'll be very much in my thoughts on Monday. But it will be all right. I'm certain of one thing; everything turns out all right in the end for those who love God."

The curate was very kind too and he wished success with a simplicity which I found extremely touching.

That Sunday I did not get up to tea, because I had been painted and bandaged ready for the following morning. I had a lot of visitors, and I spent my few periods of quiet in reading and re-reading all the letters I had received from friends who knew that the fateful day had at last arrived. People reveal their inner selves to a great extent when writing at times like these; somehow, sincerity and insincerity stand out, obvious and apparent, and all the raiment of fine words becomes completely transparent, revealing the bare emotions of the writer. Not that any of the letters were really insincere, but I felt I could gauge perfectly the exactness of sentiment felt by the person who wrote. Of course, the great majority spoke from their hearts, and there was no need for exaggeration or pretence. However, a few wrote because they felt it was their duty.

In the evening I listened to a concert broadcast from the Albert Hall. The chief work was Beethoven's 'Seventh

Symphony', which had always been a great favourite of mine.

The night nurse, a bright and attractive blonde-haired girl, came in to see me after it was finished.

"Do you like music?" she asked.

"Yes. Do you?"

"I'm mad on it. I'm having piano lessons every week. I remember when my brother and I first listened to Beethoven's Seventh; it was on a summer evening and we heard it in full on the wireless. At the end, we were so excited we were completely overcome. We both ran out into the garden and tried to recall and to hum the themes."

She opened my windows and drew back the curtains.

"You're to take sleeping tablets to-night. I'll call you at half-past five to-morrow morning, and I'll bring you some tea and toast. Try to eat it because it will be your last meal for some time. Now, do you like to be tucked up?"

"Yes, please."

"You are a baby," she laughed as she adjusted my bedclothes. "Are you worried about to-morrow?"

"A bit," I replied. "I don't want to die yet. There's so many things I still want to do."

"What sort of things?"

"Well, I've never been to the opera-house at Glyndebourne, or the Shakespeare Memorial Theatre at Stratford, and—but there's so many places I could mention."

"I see," she said. "I suppose when this sort of thing happens to you, you realise how much you've left undone."

"And how many opportunities you've missed," I added. "And how much time you've wasted all through your life."

"Try not to think too much to-night. It will only keep you awake."

She said good-night and put out my light. I turned over comfortably on my feather mattress. I was well aware that this was the last night I would be able to enjoy such ease for many weeks; that made it all the more luxurious. The drugs took effect rapidly. My mind became drowsy and without effort I crossed the border, and presently I was lost in a deep sleep.

When you are suddenly awakened at a much earlier hour than usual, your first reaction is one of bewildered annoyance. I came to my senses quickly and noticed it was dark outside, although we had only just passed Midsummer Day. Then I saw the neat figure of the blonde nurse. She was putting a breakfast tray on my bedside table. She smiled pleasantly and said in her low, rather husky voice:

"There's no need to hurry. After you've had this, you can get up and shave."

I was amazed that I was troubled so little. I ate my breakfast and quite enjoyed it. I then washed my face and hands and shaved.

She came in again to collect my tray.

"Good-bye and good luck. I'll be seeing you this evening. You'll be all right. I was looking at your documents last night; this is nothing compared with what you've been through before."

The day nurses all came in to see how I was and to wish me luck. Finally the Sister, a Scotswoman known as 'Sister Mac'. She was a grand person. Good-humoured, efficient, and capable; if ever anyone had a real flair for nursing, it was she.

Mac gave me an injection.

"This will make you a bit drowsy," she remarked. "It wouldn't be a bad idea if you could get a short sleep. They'll be up for you in about half an hour."

She drew my curtains and left the room.

I found it impossible to sleep. My brain was working so fast. I felt too hot in my bandages, operating smock and thick woollen socks which came well up over my knees. I felt thirsty too. This was the worst time of all. I tried to make my mind oblivious of all these discomforts, and of alarm, for I was experiencing a first few tremors of fear about this time. And I felt terribly alone.

Suddenly the door was thrown open. Figures in white

overalls and masks bustled in with a trolley. I climbed on to it and a nurse put some blankets over me, as I was shivering.

'This is it,' I thought, as the trolley trundled into the lift.

I wondered what Mrs. Winteringham was doing, and all my unknown friends of the Churches' Council of Healing who were praying for me on this morning. Then I thought of my relations and my acquaintances who would be wishing me well in this fateful hour.

In an instant my mind was calmed and I was filled with a great peace. When I went under the anæsthetic, all these good people would be thinking of me. The Quaker schoolmaster on my old floor had written to me that morning. "God will surely be in the Operating Theatre to-day," he had said. "He will be watching over you." I no longer felt alone. There were scores of people with me in spirit at this very moment. After all, physical presence is weak and ineffectual compared with the vital force which is generated by thought and telepathy. I felt as near to God then as I had ever felt before in my life. And this, as well as the knowledge that so many others were hoping and praying for me, gave me a buoyant confidence and a great and satisfying contentment.

The Operating Theatre was a small, bare room with the table in the centre. I climbed on to it. It was stiff and straight. I noticed the plain circular clock on the wall above my head. It was a quarter past nine. Nurses were busy with trays and implements.

A tall man walked up.

"I'm the chap who's going to put you to sleep in a moment."

He spoke kindly. I wondered why anæsthetists invariably introduced themselves in a few words of pseudo-babytalk.

It was very uncomfortable. I was lying on my back because there was no room to turn over on my side. I felt unusually flat as there was not a pillow under my head. The anæsthetist strapped a metal belt on one of my legs.

"This is the earth," he told me, "for the electrical instruments."

I was longing for the injection which would terminate everything. And then, for the first time, I realised that I could look on death without any dread. If it was God's will —then—so be it. The dark shadow had lost all its former terrors and I could regard it without flinching. My mind was at peace and I was prepared. I closed my eyes. I heard a voice saying:

"Hold out your arm. Just a little prick and you'll feel no more."

A sharp, stinging jab inside my elbow, and then, almost at once, a distant humming in my ears; a blanket of sleep drawing up from my ankles and swiftly enveloping my whole body. I had just time to think: 'Please God, let the best happen,' before my senses reeled pleasantly and decomposed into the empty void of eternity.

CHAPTER XIX

I FIRST flashed round when I was being pushed along a passage in my bed. Then I was out again. I remember the bed in the lift with orderlies and nurses standing round. Then they were wheeling me through the door of my room.

The next thing I knew, Sister Mac and Dr. Grant were injecting a blood transfusion into my foot. A nurse was waiting by my side with a chart in her hand. There was something over my mouth and I tried to tear it away. She grabbed my hand.

"No. Don't do that. You need the oxygen for a bit."

The doctor looked up.

"Is he coming round?"

Sister Mac walked up and bent over me.

"I think so. His eyes are open."

I tore the oxygen mouthpiece away again and, before they could replace it, I croaked:

"Doctor, I want you."

I was so hoarse I could hardly speak.

"I'm busy at the moment, old chap."

He was still doing something with my foot. Presently he came beside me and said:

"Well, what's wrong?"

"Was Barnaby Welch in good form?" I enquired.

A broad grin spread over the doctor's face.

"If he'd been at Lords," he said, "he would have scored a certain century."

Then he continued administering the blood transfusion. I felt terribly weak and exhausted. But I must be told what had happened. And yet, I was almost afraid to ask for details.

I lifted the mouthpiece for a moment, and this time the nurse did not try to prevent me from doing so.

"What's the time?" I asked.

"It's half-past three in the afternoon. You've been in the theatre for more than five hours. The lady who was second on the list was cursing you for keeping her waiting."

I plucked up courage.

"What did they do?" I said.

I waited in dread for a reply. There was a pause and then Dr. Grant spoke:

"It's a howling success so far. You only lost half a lung. But don't talk now. You need all your strength to recover from the tremendous ordeal which you've been through."

I remembered to thank God for his kindness. I was so tired that it was even an effort to try and take in what was going on. Then Sister Mac came over with a syringe.

"This will ease your pain a bit and send you to sleep," she said, as she gave me an injection in the arm.

Later on, when it was getting dark, they woke me up and lifted me into a sitting position. I was propped up with a deep pile of pillows.

"I'm afraid you'll have to sit up like that for over a month," said Sister Mac.

When the blonde came on duty she relieved the day nurse who was waiting with me.

"I'm so glad it went off well," she whispered as she timed my pulse. "You'll be able to go to Glyndebourne next summer after all."

211

CHAPTER XX

AT the end of two weeks I started to see visitors for short periods. I could have done so sooner, but I had decided to ask people not to visit me until then, because I thought the strain of appearing to be bright and cheerful and concealing how I really felt would be an unnecessary burden.

Mr. Barnaby Welch had expressed himself delighted with the initial results of the operation, only he feared he might have to perform another subsidiary one in a short while. However, he had gone away for a month's holiday and would make up his mind when he arrived back.

The days passed very slowly, and as soon as my strength began to return my thoughts were focused on the future. If there were no setbacks or complications I should definitely be fit enough to lead an ordinary, active life, practising as a London barrister. From the health point of view, there would now be no real obstacles, but from the professional standpoint, I had to face the unpleasant realities of the situation. By the time I might expect to recommence work I would have been away for fully eighteen months. Even before my illness I had not yet had time to make any sort of a mark for myself. And now I would definitely have to start all over again at the very beginning. At first, for perhaps two or three years at least, I would be suspect. I knew that people would be sure to say to one another:

"I wonder how long he'll last out this time."

But men forget the bad, just as quickly as they forget the good, and when I had served my probationary period I would have become absorbed into the general pattern of their lives, until at last they became oblivious of all my peculiarities.

Already sinister expressions and open warnings were creeping into the letters I was receiving from my colleagues

212

in the Temple. Was I wise to come back, they asked. The struggle was so keen, so hard, so unsparing. Some of my friends had fallen at the first hurdle; others had broken clear, only to find that the course was littered with further obstacles. It was fascinating, they said, but the going was grim and merciless.

I knew that they told me all this in kindness and solicitude, and I appreciated their feelings of sympathy. But my mind was made up. Ever since the day when I was wounded in the head I had had one principal objective—and that had been to lead a normal life in spite of my disabilities. I had a theory that, with certain obvious limitations, it was possible to overcome a severe physical handicap. You only needed a considerable amount of faith and a blind, unswerving resolution. If you prayed for help you invariably received it, and, for the rest, you had simply to put down your head, to trust in the Lord, and to tread the road which you had chosen to follow. I was not reaching for the moon or in any way striving after the unobtainable; I did not covet honours, fame, or fortune. I only wanted to work in the surroundings which I loved so much, at a job into which I could put my whole heart.

I started to read again two days after my operation, but I found at first that the strain of concentration always induced sleep. I would read about half a page, and then my eyes would close and my head would droop over my book.

I was never left alone for long. There were daily visits from the physiotherapist who was giving me arm movement and breathing exercises. Nurses came in at intervals to change my dressings and to wash me. Dr. Grant was constantly checking up on my condition. I used to look forward to the night, because it was so peaceful after the constant intrusions of the day.

At nine o'clock in the evening the night-nurse used to give me some sleeping tablets and then put out my light. I would doze for three or four hours before waking up. I was

213

always stiff and cold, and every night I developed a crick in my neck. It seemed to be impossible to sleep comfortably whilst sitting bolt-upright in bed. How I used to long for the ecstatic moment I would be able to lie flat again! When I was properly awake I would ring my bell and the nurse would bring me a cup of tea. Sometimes, when she was not busy, she stayed and talked for a while. I used to very much enjoy these whispered, drowsy conversations in the small hours of the morning. Eventually she would say:

"Now, Toby, you must try to sleep again. I have several things to do." And she would settle my bedclothes and leave me to doze on.

All the surgeons were on holiday just after my operation, so the surgical wing was not as busy as usual, and I probably received more than my fair share of attention; at any rate, far more than patients received at other seasons.

Mr. Justice Tremayne came down from London to see me, three weeks after my operation. It was on a hot, sticky evening, and he looked very tired from a long, stuffy day in the court-room. He asked me how I was feeling and also when I hoped to get up and about again. And then he came to the principal object of his visit. He was going out on the North-Eastern Circuit soon after the following Christmas, and if I felt up to it he would like me to accompany him as his marshal. I readily accepted this very kind invitation. A tour as marshal, as he pointed out, would be an excellent re-introduction to life at the Bar. The marshal is the judge's A.D.C., companion, and social secretary. He lives at the judge's lodgings and sits alongside his judge on the Bench all day long. I knew that with Mr. Justice Tremayne it would all be an interesting, instructive, and immensely enjoyable holiday. And at the end of my tour I would go back to my own Chambers to my proper work.

In due course Dr. Pearce approved the scheme and told me that from the medical point of view it sounded like an ideal rehabilitation course, always provided Mr. Welch did not want to carry out the second operation when he came back from his holiday.

However, Mr. Barnaby Welch soon put an end to my forebodings on that matter. On his first visit to the sanatorium after his return, he stood at the bottom of my bed with an X-ray film in his hand.

"Good," he said, holding the negative to the light. "Very good. No, I shan't need to do anything more with you. Well, congratulations, old man, on a very successful piece of surgery."

He good-humouredly brushed aside my words when I endeavoured to express my gratitude for all he had done for me.

"I'll get all the thanks I want," he said, "when I see you walking away, fully cured. So keep on the good work and speed your convalescence."

I was now eager to leave the surgical wing. The atmosphere was altogether different there from that on the medical floors across the way. It was impossible to escape the heavy pall of hospital gloom, when all the time patients were passing your door on stretcher-trolleys, and now and then one of the theatre staff would go by, a sinister, white-coated, masked figure. I wanted to escape from the sounds of hurrying footsteps, of low, urgent, half-heard conversations in the corridor, and the morbid, metallic clanging when the tops of oxygen cylinders were being knocked off.

I told Grant how I felt, and he agreed that the sooner I could get back to the cleaner, less troubled air of the medical side, the better. The snag was that there were no patients there who were due for operations at that moment, and the only way I could get back was by directly exchanging with somebody else. But he promised to bear it in mind and to see what could be arranged.

Then I had a rather disconcerting letter from Sebastian Shaw. He told me that he was convinced I should not return to the Bar as I had now fallen so far behind my contemporaries. He had heard, by chance, of a vacancy which

215

had just fallen in the Government Contracts Advisory Office. He had written to Mr. Justice Tremayne, who was joining with him in putting me forward for the appointment. I would become a Civil Servant, of course, but in one of the most responsible and best paid government departments.

I did not know what to think about this. I had been more than willing to do things the hard way, but I had no illusions as to what a difficult task I had set myself. And here, like a gift from the gods, was an opportunity which nobody in his senses would refuse to take. Security, a high salary, regular hours, guaranteed progressive promotion. If I was appointed to the post, my career would follow an easy, graceful and predestined course until in good time I attained the age of compulsory retirement and made my final bow with a comfortable pension, some letters of merit after my name, and perhaps, too, some prefix before it. And yet, it meant leaving the Temple for good. It meant that I would never again wear my wig and my gown and be an active participant in the most glorious and exhilarating arena where men ever matched themselves in skilful combat. Another thing, this chance coming at the exact moment it had done might have been chosen for me. It was all very well for me to foresee my life in the whirling mælstrom of the Courts, but what if my destiny lay in another field? Surely I must accept what was ordained for me with no regrets or doubts stabbing at my heart. I must keep my faith and say, with as much conviction as I could muster: 'Thy will be done. So be it.'

I wrote to Sebastian and thanked him for what he was doing. Indeed I greatly appreciated the kindness which was prompting him to take so much trouble on my behalf.

One evening when I was talking to the night-nurse, Dr. Grant came into my room. He drew back in mock embarrassment when he saw she was there.

"Oh, I'm so sorry," he said. "I see I'm interrupting something. I had heard rumours, of course, but now I know."

She coloured slightly, but joined in his tomfoolery.

"You are tactless, Doctor. We get so little time alone."

"That makes it all the harder for me to give Mr. Tobias the news I have to bring." And then turning to me he said seriously: "There's no hope of getting you back to your old abode, but you're moving to-morrow to the officers' floor."

"Poor Toby," the nurse sighed. "You can't like him very much, Dr. Grant."

The doctor grinned. "I know the patients call it 'Sister Sadie's Reform School', but I think Toby could do with a spell of discipline."

The officers' floor was reserved for serving officers and those who had held commissions in the past. It was not a popular place, as it was run on very much stricter lines than the rest of the sanatorium. Sister Sadie was an ex-Army Nursing Sister and ruled her patients and her staff with a rod of iron. Another feature which did not please the patients much was that instead of a bevy of beautiful nurses the floor was tended by a robust squad of male Army nursing orderlies.

This news did not displease me at all. Any move would be welcome, and whilst I regretted not going back to the place which I knew, I had heard that underneath Sister Sadie's stern countenance lay an unfailing sense of humour and a heart of gold. And anyhow, it was a definite fact that for an inexplicable reason some of the serving officers seemed invariably to be rather less co-operative and slightly more irresponsible than the ordinary civilian patients.

I was taken to my new room in a wheel-chair the following morning. The floor was a large one running almost the entire length of the building. There were over thirty patients on it, some in single rooms and some in double rooms. There was also a small three-bedded dormitory at the end, which was affectionately called the 'rat-hole'. Sister Sadie chose people for the double rooms with the utmost care, and she was usually successful in selecting two patients who could get on well together. I had feared that

I would have to share a room, but she moved me into a single one and in fact I remained by myself until the day I was discharged.

I soon found out there was none of the sociability and helpfulness on the officers' floor which was such a feature of the remainder of Hedgely. No neighbours came in to see me, and those who had the communal jobs of collecting and delivering never bothered to stay for a chat. However, I was starting to get up and Dr. Grant had told me that I would pass quickly through the grades as the doctors were so pleased with my post-operative progress. I found Sister Sadie very charming and always anxious to do everything possible for her patients' comfort, though I was irked by the special floor rules and regulations and the notices all over the walls. Shortly after my arrival the Sister asked me to take over the duties of Floor Representative, and I willingly agreed. I realised I was becoming rather bored and irritable. I was, at the time, going through an anticlimactic phase when everything seemed shallow and listless. Of course, I knew it would pass off as soon as I left the sanatorium.

I ran into trouble quickly when I arrived on my new floor. I had been sleeping very badly over on the surgical wing, partly because I was forcing myself as far as possible to do without sleeping drugs. After my lights were put out at ten o'clock on my first night in my new room, I found it impossible to relax because some wireless set was blaring out a few doors up the passage. It was still going after midnight, vexing and tantalising in its persistence. At last, in desperation, I rang for the night-nurse. It was fully ten minutes before she bustled in.

"What's the matter?" she enquired brusquely.

I pointed out that there was a rule at Hedgely that wirelesses were switched off at ten o'clock and patients who wished to continue listening in were supposed to use the sanatorium earphones.

"I can't hear any wireless," she replied, cocking her head

218

and pretending to listen. "I'll tell you what," she went on brightly, "I'll get you a sleeping tablet."

I flatly declined her offer, and after further heated words between us she walked out in a huff. She was not a member of the regular sanatorium staff, but she had been temporarily attached from a small provincial hospital for a specialised course of training.

She was a girl who took no interest in her job. A buxom, good-looking, though a somewhat over-blown, type, she always ruined herself by putting a dreadful mass of clumsily applied make-up on her face. Owing to the muck which she plastered round her eyes she was always known as 'Mascara Maggie'. I think she imagined herself as being one of those glamorous Hollywood nurses on the films.

Maggie, during her short spell of night duty, had had half a dozen ardent love affairs with various patients. Her latest intrigue, I learned later, was with the owner of the very loud wireless set. Apparently she had been sitting in his room drinking cocktails and enjoying a programme of late dance music when I had rung to complain about the noise.

Most of us breathed a sigh of relief when Maggie was taken off night duty and posted away from our floor. However, she still stole back every evening to visit her boyfriend, and there was a rather amusing incident when she was almost caught in his room. I think the Night Sister had a pretty shrewd idea what was going on and that evening she waited until after 'Lights out', and then executed a lightning raid. Maggie heard her footsteps approaching and succeeded in slipping out on to the balcony. She stood there for three-quarters of an hour in the pouring rain before she thought it safe to return. Apparently she looked a sorry sight, with her drenched hair straggling over her soggy clothes and her dissolving grease-paint oozing and smearing down her cheeks. It was rumoured that the owner of the troublesome radio never again felt the same about Maggie after that night.

The officers' floor had none of the tranquillity I had

219

always encountered before at Hedgely. The orderlies were all young National Service lads who used to stamp about whistling, shouting and singing. When Sister Sadie was off duty the whole place was always in a state of uproar. There were two patients sharing a room at the end of the corridor who added to the bedlam by beating drums, sound-motor-car horns, and twirling rattles. They were both bored stiff with being in bed so long, and gave vent to their repressed energies in ways more befitting a boys' kindergarten school than a convalescent home for the sick. Their neighbours, a lot of whom were recovering from severe operations, did not find this pastime so amusing. It had the effect of making me even keener than I had been to leave Hedgely for good.

Sebastian had asked me to write to Mr. Ernest Twittering, the head of the Government Contracts Advisory Office. I did so a short while after my move to the officers' floor. A few days later I received a long reply. It was such a pompous letter it made me shudder. First of all I was reproved for addressing the great man as 'Dear Mr. Twittering'. In chilling terms he remarked:

"I address you as 'Dear Tobias' and you should address me as 'Dear Twittering' because we are both members of the Bar, and you know that members of the Bar, no matter how great their disparities of age and standing, always call each other by their surnames without any prefixes."

He went on to tell me how terribly clever all the members of his staff were. "We consider ourselves, and very rightly so, to be among the élite, both in intellect and in all-round efficiency, of the entire Civil Service. It is my task to see that our very high standard is maintained. When you come to see me I shall be judging you by our own exclusive standards which are very far above the ordinary."

A man from my new Chambers was visiting me when Twittering's letter arrived. I gave it to him to read.

"Silly, inflated ass," he muttered disrespectfully. Then he frowned.

220

"Toby, I don't like the idea of your getting mixed up with that crew," he said.

"Why not?" I asked.

"Well, the jobs are excellent, but it's not the Bar. No matter how much old Twittering tries to hang on to his status as a barrister, the fact is he's a ruddy Civil Servant now and has no connection whatsoever with the Bar as we know it. And anyway, I've been making enquiries about his department of super-men. There may be several rather awkward and tiresome customers in it."

"What sort of people?"

"They're probably all men, Ernest included, who have tried the Bar without any great success. Mind you, they're not fools; far from it. They're mostly purely academic lawyers; probably that's why none of them could quite make the grade. A mass of theory and book knowledge and a hopeless inability to apply it in practice. You must know the sort of thing. And now they have settled in their comfortable niches and they're very pleased with themselves, but somehow they feel a trifle sour at the same time. They're very proud of being members of the Bar, and yet they know in their hearts that they were not too good at the principal job for which barristers exist."

I was full of apprehension as well. Twittering's letter was couched in a cold formality which I found distinctly repellent. There was about it none of the easy camaraderie and none of the good-humoured cheerfulness which characterised the relationships of the Temple. And yet, I made myself think, style is often very deceptive; probably Twittering would be completely different in real life.

I wrote back assuring him that I would let him know when I was discharged from Hedgely, so that he could arrange for an interview. By then most of my old friends had left the sanatorium. In the early autumn of that year it was dark, damp and gloomy. The patients sitting in the lounges huddled silently round the fires, longing and praying for the day of their release. It was all so bleak and cheerless. Of course, the various batches of patients passing through the sanatorium varied enormously from one month to another in their collective interest. All the staff were agreed that we happened to form a particularly dull crop, but they accepted us with a sigh of resignation. After all, they could not expect a vintage yield every season. But I found personally the dearth of good company made the time drag terribly.

At last I was allowed up to breakfast, and a few days later I was taking my half-mile test. There was none of the exhilaration I had felt on the first occasion I had been through all this; at times I felt as if I was only re-treading the forest path in order to get back to the main road at the point at which I had lost my direction.

Someone who was also on his second visit to Hedgely said to me on one of our morning walks:

"Have you ever played 'Snakes and Ladders'?"

"Why yes," I replied, "but not for years now. Not since I was a child."

"It's been rather like that for us," he went on. "We had got well on the way when the dice landed us on an unlucky square and we had to go back right to the start."

"It may look like that," I said, "but perhaps it's a false impression. Life never stands still, and the clocks are never really put back. There is always an inevitable movement forward."

I spoke those words as much to convince myself as to refute his theory.

When we returned to the sanatorium I went to my room with my newspaper. I flicked through the pages, but I was not reading, my mind had returned to its usual topic of 'How long more?', and was busy with the customary computations of the minimum and the maximum number of days that could possibly elapse before my release.

Suddenly I noticed a headline.

"High Court Judge Taken Ill."

I read on:

222

"Mr. Justice Tremayne, the High Court judge, is desperately ill in a country nursing home. He collapsed yesterday and his condition last night was stated to be critical."

During the following week I was discharged from Hedgely.

CHAPTER XXI

I ARRIVED in Whitehall much too early for my interview, so I walked down to Parliament Square and along past the Palace of Westminster.

It was a bright morning and the sun shone out over the magnificent stability of Big Ben. I stood still and watched the busy London crowd, scampering, scurrying, and hustling, as though the world might come to a sudden end before they would have time to finish their essential errands. At that moment I liked them for being what they were. People in a mass were nondescript and impersonal, but if you could only pick some of them out, or turn a spotlight on a few of them, they were transformed into personalities full of interest. I looked at various individuals as they hurried by. I stared rudely and unashamedly. After all, until a week or so ago I had been hidden away from crowds and isolated from ordinary people for many months. They knew I was watching them, but they did not seem to resent my behaviour. I certainly looked respectable enough with my dark overcoat, my black hat, and my rolled umbrella. They probably guessed that I was just one of those peculiar people who are interested in humanity as such. That, I reflected, was why I had chosen to become a barrister. That was why I had found my spiritual home in the Courts of law.

I looked at my watch. It was seven minutes to twelve. I started to stroll back slowly up the entire length of Whitehall.

I found the Government Contracts Office down a turning near the Admiralty Arch, and I told the commissionaire the name of the person whom I had come to see. He retired to a cubby-hole to put through a call on the internal telephone. Five minutes later he was leading me up a single flight of stairs and down a wide corridor into a waiting-room where I hung my hat and coat. Then a girl came and showed me into a large, comfortable room where Mr. Ernest Twittering was standing warming himself in front of a blazing coal-fire.

He was an exceptionally tall man with a completely bald head. He peered at me for a moment or two through the thick lenses of his spectacles, then advanced towards me with outstretched hand.

"I'm glad to meet you, Tobias, after all I've heard about you."

He asked me to sit down in an arm-chair which had been placed in readiness, and he himself sat behind his desk. For several minutes he remained silent, eyeing me intently.

I glanced round the room. It was furnished in a far more luxurious style than any barrister's Chambers I had ever seen, but it was definitely arranged in the style usually adopted in the Temple. The imitation was obvious enough to bear all the crudeness of a parody. It reminded me of an Old Etonian socialist I knew who always adopted a very artificial Cockney accent whenever he addressed meetings in the East End of London.

My gaze came back to Twittering. He had the frigid, dispassionate appearance of the prim intellectual. His face was thin and inanimate, and his eyes humourless and cold. He wore that unfortunate look of a man who was constantly getting nasty smells which the other people around him were too insensitive to notice.

"Tobias," he said suddenly, "are you brilliant?"

"No," I answered frankly. "I don't think I am."

He sighed. "Do you really think you could cope with the sort of work we do here?"

"Mr. Justice Tremayne and Sebastian Shaw apparently think I could, and I'm certainly not prepared to say that anything's beyond me until I've tried it."

"You see, you have no academic distinctions to speak of. All my men come here with a reputation for scholarship.

225

You didn't even take a good degree after the war, did you?"

"No," I replied. And then I added: "There were certain difficulties. I had been wounded."

He waved his hand. "I know. I know all about that. You had a gallant war record, but I must not allow that to blind my judgment. I'm only interested now in your qualifications for this difficult and highly intricate work."

"I'm afraid I'll have to stand or fall by what others have said about me."

He took up two letters which were lying in front of him. "Tremayne and Shaw speak of you very highly. But it all boils down to one thing, that you made a fairly promising start at the Bar, and you know as well as I do that you don't need brains at the Bar. You may need other qualities, but definitely not brains. What concerns me is that you've done nothing in your life which betrays any real scholastic brilliance."

I made no answer. He tapped the desk thoughtfully with a pencil.

"Did you know Tremayne well?"

I said: "Yes. Well enough to admire him as much as any man I've ever met."

"I hear he probably won't recover. And even if he does he'll never be fit enough to return to the Bench. It's a great shame. I suppose you're very keen to come to my department?"

I hesitated. "Well. If I liked the work. I know it's an excellent job."

He left his desk and stood leaning against the mantelpiece with his back to the fire.

"It's more than an excellent job, much more. We are among the élite of the Civil Service. We start off at a salary that would make any junior barrister green with envy. You realise that, don't you?"

I answered loyally: "Nobody in their right senses goes to the Bar these days in the hope of making a lot of money."

He looked surprised. "What, then?"

,"There is something about the life," I said.

"As I was saying," he went on, "if I could see my way to recommending your acceptance to the Selection Board, you would straightaway be paid a salary far in excess of anything you could possibly earn at the Bar during the next few years. But it goes much further than that. You would be the youngest man here. That means in time you would be almost certain to rise to my position. Do you understand? At some time in the future you would stand in my shoes."

He drew himself up and paused dramatically. Almost unconsciously my eyes travelled down to his feet, which he had placed side by side as he was speaking. His shoes were black, shiny and expensive. He was waiting for me to answer and in the awkward silence he followed the line of my gaze. In an instant he saw what I was looking at and he realised the reason why. He turned away, puzzled and embarrassed. I felt rather guilty, I wanted to laugh and I longed for him to burst out laughing too. But he did not.

After a few moments he faced me again and prepared to say something, checked himself, and muttered: "No, perhaps not."

He sat down at his desk again. He did not care now. Neither did I. I knew he had decided that I was definitely unsuitable. He had not ever really thought I would do, and the shoes episode had definitely clinched the matter.

I was quite relieved when he started to talk of other things. About Hedgely, the war, and the general news of the day. Eventually, at one o'clock, he rose.

"Well, Tobias, it was nice of you to come along. But you understand how it is."

"Yes, I understand perfectly."

As he was showing me out of the door he said:

"What will you do with yourself now that this hasn't come off?"

"I'll go back," I said.

227

"Then I wish you the very best of luck," he said as he shook my hand.

I thanked him and went away.

At the booking-office of Westminster Underground Station I put down a threepenny-piece on the counter.

"Temple, please," I said to the clerk.

"Temple," he repeated casually as he handed me a ticket.

Temple! Temple! Temple! I wanted to hear the word spoken again and again, because it had such a wonderful, magical sound in my ears. The Temple was my Mecca.

As I stood on the platform waiting for a train, I was feeling blissfully happy. I kept telling myself I had failed to get the job. I had been turned down flat, and now the road seemed to stretch before me so clear and so obvious that never before in my life had I felt quite so certain that there was only one possible course for me to follow.

EPILOGUE

THE bus was almost empty when I jumped on to it at
Chancery Lane. I sat down on one of the lengthways seats
just inside the entrance. The conductor was counting his
tickets and filling in numbers on a form. Every now and
then he licked a stub of pencil, and the whole time he was
humming a tune under his breath.

If there was not much traffic in the Strand, I thought, I
should not be so very late. Anyhow, I was lucky to be
going at all as I had nearly been held up at London Sessions
for the whole of the afternoon. Fortunately for me the
jury had reached their verdict half an hour ago. I had been
down in the cells, speaking to the little Pole I was defending,
when the prison officer had given me the news that they
were coming back. I hurried up the steps and through the
dock as the last jurors were filing into their places. I
scanned their faces, but it was not any use, for in no way
did they betray their thoughts.

"Members of the jury, are you agreed on your verdict?"
the clerk asked.

"We are," said the foreman.

"Do you find the prisoner 'guilty' or 'not guilty'?"

"We find him 'not guilty'."

The trial had lasted three days. It had been a hard, up-
hill struggle all the way. And now it was all over.

I stood up. This was always a proud and happy moment
for any defending counsel.

"Milord. I apply for the prisoner to be discharged."

"Yes, let him go," murmured the judge, and the Pole
shuffled out of the dock to join his wife and his friends.

Afterwards in the robing-room the barrister who had
appeared for the prosecution came up and patted me on the
back.

229

"Well done, old chap. That was a good victory."

In my day-dreams I suddenly became aware of the conductor's unobtrusive singing. He saw me looking at him
and grinned.

"Remember it?"

I smiled back. "You're a bit out of date, aren't you?"

"Yes. It must have been about the winter of 1939-40."
He started to sing again:

> "When we go walking in the park at night,
> The darkness is a boon.
> Who cares if we're without a light?
> They can't black out the moon."

He stopped and sighed:

"Lord, how it brings back memories for me."

I said: "It does for me too."

The first winter of the war. An ill-lit railway station.
The transient shadows of the people who passed by, their
low, muffled voices and the odd, disjointed overheard
phrases. The bulky, padded form of a soldier in equipment with his arm round a girl, clasping her so tightly that
she bent over under his weight. The pathetic scene in the
dingy, sullen buffet when women, their good-byes finished,
dabbed their eyes over cups of luke-warm tea and told one
another, unbelievingly, that it would not be for long now.
One could go on interminably re-creating those ghostly
images from the past.

The conductor stuck the pencil behind his ear and put
away the form.

"Where to, skipper?" he asked.

"Charing Cross, please."

"That'll be twopence," he said, punching a ticket.

He went on up the bus collecting some other fares. Then
he came back again and stood at the entrance.

"They were good times," he said reminiscently. "There's
a sort of bond among those who lived through them. When

I see the young men and women coming along these days,
I sometimes think that there's no link whatever between
me and them."

"Perhaps we don't realise we're growing so much older,"
I remarked.

"Well, maybe you're right there. But I feel young
enough for all that. I suppose these youngsters look on us
as old fogeys. And before long another lot will grow up,
and they'll look on them as being old fogeys in their turn.
Each generation seems to be quite unconnected with the
last. It beats me. There's no—no——"

"Continuity?" I suggested.

"Yes, that's the word. There's no continuity about it all.
We had different ideas to the present lot. There's a proper
barrier separating us and them. And it will be the same
with each new lot that comes along, for ever and ever.
Amen."

The bus drew up at the Aldwych stop and half a dozen
people came on board, putting an end to our conversation.

I left the bus outside Charing Cross Station and walked
quickly up Duncannon Street. It was the first Wednesday
in the month, and on the first Wednesday in every calendar
month the Churches' Council of Healing held a special
service in St. Martin's-in-the-Fields at three o'clock in the
afternoon.

The large church was crowded when I arrived, and the
service had already started. The sidesman led me to a
vacant place in the rearmost pew. I knelt down and
thanked God for bringing me through my illness and my
operation.

The atmosphere in the building was warm and friendly.
I felt immediately that I was one of a united community
which comprised all types and all ages. I wondered if this
was the essence of the continuity for which the bus conductor had searched in vain.

Then I realised how a phase in my life was now completed. I had suffered disablement and I had overcome it.

231

I had undergone a critical operation and I had survived it. I had always had faith in the Lord and my faith had been rewarded. I had, at last, been able to take up the life for which I longed—the life of an unknown, junior barrister. Other struggles lay ahead, further setbacks, further achievements. But the most important part—perhaps the only important part—of my life was over. I had demonstrated to myself, and to any others who wished to observe, that the love and mercy of God is boundless and infinite for all those who seek it.

My story was indeed only half written, but what lay in the future did not count. Probably I was never destined to make any mark in the world; probably the fickle, shifting sands of time would efface my footprints altogether in the moment when I had passed by. If everybody lives for only one essential purpose, then the design of my existence was fulfilled. The rest did not really matter.

I looked round at the people about me. Some were ill; some were crippled; some had come merely to pray for a sick relative or acquaintance. All were joined together in asking for Divine intercession as an answer to their own and their neighbours' prayers. I thought of my very ill companions at Hedgely, and of Mr. Justice Tremayne, one of the finest and the best, who was still in a desperate condition at a London nursing home.

I knew that there were others in that congregation who were not praying for the relief of any physical infirmity, but who were in need of help all the same. For without exception we all have some sort of a cross to bear. It may arise from a fear, a doubt, a worry, a hidden unhappiness, a jealousy, a frustration, or from a host of other causes. But it is always there in the life of every one of us. And we all need protection and comfort. I know for an absolute certainty that the same fount of love and assistance which was ready for me in my hour of need is also accessible for all people on earth, no matter how great are their troubles.

In a way it is far easier to be a good Christian when one

232

is in a hospital bed fighting for recovery. In the outside world ambition, covetousness, avarice and pride are constantly shooting their poisoned arrows into our hearts. If only we could remember how very little it all matters, and how dimly the feeble lights of our individual successes shine amid the whole vastness of the firmament. The only acquisition in life which is worth while is peace of mind, and the great and unique happiness which flows from its possession. I have often noticed how false and how ephemeral are our manufactured happinesses, and I have compared them with the mental serenity of the few people I know who have discovered the marvellous, lasting peace of God—the peace which passes all understanding.

The blind ministrant announced a hymn and everyone rose and started to sing. The words were strangely in accordance with my thoughts:

> "When I survey the wondrous Cross,
> On which the Prince of Glory died,
> My richest gain I count but loss,
> And pour contempt on all my pride."